# TWICE DAILY AFTER MEALS

In aid of the Royal Medical Benevolent Fund
- a charity which supports doctors in need and their dependants

This edition published by the Medi-Derm Company Limited,
25 Highfield Road, Northwood, HA6 1EU

ISBN 0-9539408-0-2

Cover design by The Creative Lynx Partnership

Supported by a donation from Leo Pharmaceuticals
and a generous grant from Wyeth Laboratories

# TWICE DAILY AFTER MEALS

## A SELECTION OF THE WIT AND WISDOM OF THE CELEBRATED

Edited and compiled by
S.K.Goolamali MD, FRCP
Consultant Dermatologist
Northwick Park and St Mark's Hospitals,
Harrow, Middlesex

# Preface

THIS BOOK IS DEDICATED to the Royal Medical Benevolent Fund - RMBF - a charity founded for doctors and their dependants who fall on hard times. It is a sad fact that hundreds of doctors and their families are forced to live on the poverty line after a serious illness or accident. Professional pride and a perception of loss of dignity prevent many from seeking help when timely assistance could make all the difference. The RMBF exists to support both young and old - the elderly with inadequate pensions, widows with children or doctors unable to work as a result of injury or physical or mental handicap.

All the royalties from this book are to be donated to the RMBF. I am deeply indebted to the authors, all busy personalities who gave their services without hesitation and without fee. Their many anecdotes and recollections exemplify wit, humour and much human experience. The pieces range from short jokes as might be used in an after-dinner speech to abstracts from a personal common-place book, a record of a true event to a fictional story.

**Twice Daily After Meals** took more than two years from inception to production. During its formulation two valued contributors Professor David Baum, then President of the Royal College of Paediatrics and Child Health and Mr Harry "Nero" Blacker, cartoonist extraordinaire, sadly died. David Baum tragically died of a heart attack during a charity cycle race and Harry Blacker of cancer. Both their contributions are included in the book as they had wished and as a tribute to their lives and talent.

TDAM as it is now affectionately dubbed is to be taken in measured quantities during periods of rest or recreation. It is designed to uplift the spirit and banish melancholy and if it succeeds in making you smile or give you food for thought please buy another copy for a friend!

S.K.GOOLAMALI

# Acknowledgments

THERE ARE MANY PEOPLE to whom I owe a debt of gratitude for helping me in the preparation of this book that to name some will be to commit the sin of omitting others. I apologise to those I have unwittingly excluded.

To all included below I give my thanks for their advice, generosity and the many suggestions regarding contributors to the book. Their encouragement and assistance has undoubtedly improved and strengthened a project which started as a promising idea and hopefully has ended as an interesting read.

In alphabetical order:

Mr Michael Baber
Miss Sue Crossley
Mr Tim Edwards
Mr Iain Fyfe
Dr Clive Handler
Mr Derek Heasman
Mr Christopher Kelly
Mr Joe Kerridge
Dr Malcolm Phillips
Sir Rodney Sweetnam
Mr Neil Tolley
Mr Stuart Wilson

An enterprise of this kind could not have matured without the unstinting help of my wife Alma, my daughter Nina and my son Sacha. I wish to record my fondest thanks to them.

All the authors were invited to submit original material and personal photographs. However, a few sent previously published copy and here permission was sought from copyright holders and due acknowledgement has been made in the text where appropriate. The editor and the publishers would like to take this opportunity to record our thanks to all these contributors. If omissions or errors regarding copyright are brought to our attention these will gladly be corrected in a future edition.

# Contents

# Dr Douglas Acres

*Douglas Acres has been a GP, a JP, and an LP (General Practitioner, a Justice of the Peace and a Lay Pastor) for the best part of the last 40 years. He qualified at the London Hospital in 1949, and was appointed to the Rochford Bench in Essex in 1958, serving as its Chairman for 14 years.*

*He was Chairman of the Council of the Magistrates' Associations from 1984-87, and since then has been a Vice-President. His involvement in medicine and the magistracy were found useful in his appointment to several committees and working parties, such as the Butler Committee on Mentally Abnormal Offenders, the Parole Board, the Barclay Committee on the Role and Task of the Social Worker, and the Interdepartmental Committee on Alcoholism.*

*In 1981 he was awarded the OBE and promoted to CBE in 1987 for services to the magistracy. During his period on the Butler Committee, with the aid of a Cropwood Fellowship, conducted a follow-up of those discharged from Special Hospitals directly into the community.*

*On his retirement from General Medical Practice in 1984, he became Lay Pastor of Battlebridge Free Church, retiring because of fibrosing alveolitis in 1998.*

# The Perplexed Pharmacist

Shortly after commencing in general practice in 1953 I had a woman patient with a severe cancer phobia. I initiated many tests, all of which proved negative, and reported the findings to her, saying that it was not possible to prove that she did not suffer from cancer, but that all the indications were that she was a very healthy woman. Being a lay preacher as well as a GP I advised her to go home to read the Epistle to the Romans, chapter 8, verse 39: to the effect that "nothing shall be able to separate us from the love of God". As an aid to memory I wrote on a prescription: Rom 8: 39. A few minutes later the local pharmacist rang me, starting his conversation, as was invariably the case, with "I say", and continued, "what is this Rom 8:39? I can't find it any pharmacopoeia". I was able to assure him that this was intended for self-medication, not for him to dispense.

# A Mistaken Request

In the early hours of one morning in February, during the 1953 East Coast flood disaster, when I was serving as a National Service Medical Officer in the RAF, I had a call from Canvey Island, requesting, as I thought, for a "doc right away". I arrived on the island and after some difficulty arrived at the agreed spot, but no one seemed to know what was required of me. After some contemplation the caller declared, "No, we sent for a DUCW, (an amphibious vehicle) not a doc!"

# Richard Adams

*Richard Adams son of a country doctor, Evelyn George Adams, FRCS and Lillian Rose Adams was raised in Berkshire and Hampshire. He graduated MA from Oxford in Modern History and entered the Civil Service. In 1966, he wrote 'Watership Down' which he originally told to his daughters to while away a long car journey. 'Watership Down' was published in November 1972 and awarded the Carnegie Medal and the Guardian Award for Children's Fiction for 1972.*

*He retired from the Civil Service and has since written a number of books including 'Shardik' (1974); 'Nature through the Seasons' (with Max Hooper, 1975); 'The Plague Dogs' (1977); 'Nature Day and Night' (with Max Hooper, 1978); 'Voyage through the Antarctic' (with Ronald Lockley, 1982); 'The Bureaucats' (1985) and most recently, 'The Outlandish Knight' (2000).*

*He is married to Barbara Acland and has two daughters, Juliet and Rosamond.*

# Captain Wilcox and the Explosive Cigarette

In 1941, I was a subaltern in 3rd Corps Petrol Park, RASC. A number of the subalterns (of whom I was one) in the Officers' Mess decided that the time had come for us to play a practical joke on the Workshops Officer, Captain Wilcox. Captain Wilcox was a decent chap and a good sport whom we all liked, but he was a bit inclined to hold forth and pontificate on any subject which particularly took his fancy.

Our joke was to take the form of an explosive cigarette. For this joke it is necessary to have a cork-tipped cigarette, to make sure that the victim lights it at the right end. About half the tobacco in the cigarette is gently prised out with a needle, after which a child's "pink cap", intended for a toy pistol, is inserted, and the tobacco put neatly back again. I was detailed for the task of actually proffering the cigarette to the Captain.

The following evening, there was an ENSA party performing for the troops, and of course they were invited to the Officers' Mess afterwards for drinks and snacks. Upon their arrival, the ladies went upstairs "to powder their noses", while the male performers joined us in the Mess. I had my cigarette case filled with the appropriate brand of cork-tipped cigarette. Sure enough, Captain Wilcox took his usual place, on the hearth rug and back to the fire, and began setting the world to rights. I was sitting directly in front of him, on a sofa. I opened my case and pushed the "doctored" cigarette forward. I then proffered the case towards Captain Wilcox, saying "Cigarette, Wilkie?". He took it casually and with thanks and lighted it. Then he continued to pontificate. He had been going about two more minutes when the pink cap went up with a bang and the cigarette flayed out like a sort of small mop. Wilkie didn't drop it, being a man of firm nerve. It was between his fingers and he brought his hand round to his face, looked at the remains of the cigarette and said loudly "Well, bugger me!".

At this moment the ladies came into the Mess. He had not seen them because they were behind a drawing-room screen, set up by the door to protect against draughts. But they heard him all right - all of them! We subalterns, of course, were doubled up with helpless laughter for about two minutes on end.

This is the funniest and most successful practical joke in which I have ever taken part.

# Earl Alexander of Tunis

Photograph courtesy of Desmond O'Neill Features

*Shane William Desmond Alexander was created Second Earl in 1952. He is a Director of the International Hospitals Group and associated companies and of the Pathfinder Financial Corporation, Toronto. He was a Lieutenant in the Irish Guards from which he retired in 1958. He was educated at Ashbury College, Ottawa, Canada and Harrow. He became A Lord in Waiting (Government Whip) in 1974 and was president of the British-American-Canadian Associates 1989-1994. He is Chairman of the Canada Memorial Foundation and also Patron of the British Tunisian Society. He received the Order of the Republic of Tunisia in 1995.*

# Three Times a Lady

Can you hear me at the back? I ask only because a friend of mine thought his wife was going deaf. He decided that the best way of testing her hearing was when she was not expecting it.

One evening he came home to see her sitting by the fireplace reading a newspaper with her back to him. Now was the time to test her hearing. He stood in the doorway and said in a normal voice "Can you hear me?" There was no reply. He went into the middle of the room and said in a normal voice "Can you hear me?" Still no reply. He went up and stood behind her and repeated in a normal voice "Can you hear me?"

She lowered her paper and looked up at him "For the third time, yes I can".

# Peter Alliss

*Peter Alliss was born in Berlin, the son of a famous British Professional, Percy Alliss, one of Britain's leading professionals, 1920-39.*

*Peter Alliss represented Great Britain and Ireland 8 times in Ryder Cup competitions and England 10 times in the World Cup. He was twice Captain of the Professional Golfers' Association and was the first President of the European Women's Professional Golfers' Association, also past President of the British Greenkeepers' Association.*

*During his UK playing career, he won the PGA Championship three times, the Open Championships of Spain, Italy, Portugal and Brazil, plus twenty other European victories.*

*Peter is recognised around the world for his television commentaries for ABC in the United States and the BBC in Europe, but has also worked for the Australian and Canadian Broadcasting Corporations. He was the host of 140 Pro Celebrity Golf television programmes made by the BBC between the years 1974 and 1988, and was also the host of another very successful series entitled "Around with Alliss". His most recent television series, "A Golfer's Travels", is still being shown on worldwide television.*

*His involvement with golf course architecture goes back over 30 years. With his first partner, David Thomas, they created over 50 golf courses, including The Belfrey, which is now the home of the British Professional Golfers' Association and where the Ryder Cup has been played on numerous occasions; the Seve Club in Japan; La Baule in Brittany; the Lansdowne Course at Blairgowrie in Scotland; Old Thorns in Hampshire and Yamasukra on the Ivory Coast.*

*At this time, his Company, Peter Alliss - Golf Limited, is working on courses throughout Europe and the Middle East.*

# The 19th Hole

The scene St Andrews, dreadful day, wind blowing in from the sea, rain like 303 bullets, but a lone American had made the pilgrimage to play round the Old Course. There was one caddy left, "auld Tam". They set off, they were of course wet through by the time they got to the 1st green. On the 2nd tee the old American took a bottle of Scotch from his bag, took a swig and plodded manfully on. Hole after hole went by, every 2 or 3 holes he had a swig out the whisky bottle. The play was not good, the conversation pretty well nil, the umbrella had been blown inside out.

Then they reached the turn for home, so did the wind, so once more they were battling back into all the dire forces of nature. Eventually they reached the 16th tee and the American said to auld Tam "Isn't there a dry spot on this godforsaken course". Auld Tam looked up bleary eyed and said "Aye sir, you could try the back of my throat".

# Jeffrey Archer

*Jeffrey Archer was born in London, brought up in Somerset and went on to Oxford, where he was President of the University Athletics Club, and went on to run the 100 yards in 9.6 seconds for Great Britain in 1966.*

*Elected to the GLC in 1966, three years later at the age of 29, he became Member of Parliament for Louth. After five years he resigned and wrote his first novel, "Not A Penny More Not a Penny Less". Now, having written ten books, three plays, and four collections of short stories, he is published in thirty two languages and sixty four countries, with international sales passing one hundred and twenty million copies. His new play, "The Accused", in which he plays the title role, opened at London's Haymarket Theatre on 5th December 2000.*

*Jeffrey Archer is a former Deputy Chairman of the Conservative Party, and was made a Life Peer in the Queen's Birthday Honours List of 1992. He is an amateur auctioneer, conducting some 50 charity auctions a year, and in 1991 he co-ordinated the Campaign for Kurdish Relief which raised over fifty seven million pounds for the Kurdish people. His new novel, "Serendipity", will be published in 2001.*

# Childhood Memory

As a schoolboy, one of my more memorable experiences is of a journey I took during a school holiday, from Weston-super-Mare in Somerset to Leeds in Yorkshire. The purpose of the journey was to spend Christmas with an Aunt and Uncle who were school teachers in North Alleren and as I had never before travelled beyond Bristol or Bridgwater, I looked forward to the day with much anticipation and relish. My Grandmother was one of those early drivers who had not acquired a licence, and had she ever taken the test she would have undoubtedly frightened the examiner out of his wits.

We left Weston-super-Mare in the morning in a large green Morris Oxford. My Grandmother drove, my Grandfather and Mother in the back while I had the honour of sitting in the front, decades before anyone had thought of seatbelts. My Grandmother like myself, rarely travelled beyond the environs of Weston-super-Mare and for her the roundabout was a new fangled invention which she had not encountered before. We discovered the first one some seven miles outside my home town, over which she happily drove straight across the middle and carried on in a northerly direction. We encountered twenty three such obstacles set unnecessarily in our progress, on our route between Weston-super-Mare and Leeds and my Grandmother crossed all of them in a manner which would have pleased Hannibal.

On arrival in Leeds, my Grandfather who had learnt several years before not to speak, my Mother who was not listened to when she did, and I who did not murmur a word, breathed more than a sigh of relief when we eventually arrived at my Uncle's front door in one piece. Once safely on the premises, I ventured the innocent question of my Grandmother, "surely one should go around roundabouts and not across them?", to which she replied with British certainty "certainly not. What you must understand young man, is that they will never catch on", a degree of logic with which I am quite unable to find fault.

We returned home by train.

# Professor David Baum

*John David Baum was born in Birmingham. His routine of hard work instilled in him by his beloved parents, immigrants from Eastern Europe, began in his school days. After qualifying at Birmingham Medical School, he developed a career in Paediatrics and moved quickly into neonatal medicine. After a period in Denver, Colorado, he became one of the leaders of British Neonatology at the John Radcliffe Hospital, Oxford.*

*Baum developed a special interest in the nutrition of babies. He was awarded the Guthrie Prize for the most outstanding young paediatrician by the British Paediatric Association. His interest in diabetes in the young began at Oxford. As an advocate of treating the whole child together with the child's family, he introduced novel strategies into the care of diabetics. He was elected the first President of the Royal College of Paediatrics and Child Health. His contacts with Mikhail Gorbachev led to a link between Bristol where he worked and the Filatoff Hospital in Moscow. The Medical Aid for Palestinians Project was another he was involved in and he helped develop facilities for young doctors in this divided region.*

*David Baum stayed true to a parable about the importance of the individual. This parable is published in this volume, as he wished.*

# The Parable of the Starfish

As the old man walked the beach at dawn, he noticed a young man ahead of him picking up starfish and slinging them into the sea. Finally catching up with the youth, he asked him why he was doing this. The answer was that the stranded starfish would die if left until the morning sun. "But the beach goes on for miles and there are millions of starfish" countered the other. "How can your effort make any difference?" The young man looked at the starfish in his hand then threw it to safety in the waves. "It makes a difference to this one", he said.

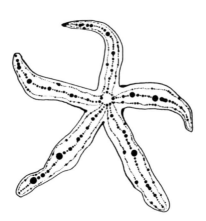

# Sir Richard Bayliss

*Richard Bayliss KCVO, MD, FRCP, is Consulting Physician to the Lister Hospital, London. He was Physician to the Queen 1970 to 1981 and Head of Her Majesty's Medical Household 1973 to 1981.*

*Previous appointments include Vice-President of Private Patients Plan (PPP) and Consultant Physician to King Edward VII Hospital for Officers. He has been an Examiner in Medicine for Cambridge and Oxford Universities and Examiner for the MRCP (UK). He has been a member of the Council of the Royal College of Physicians, London and its Second Vice-President.*

*His publications include 'Thyroid Disease: The Facts' (3rd edition, 1998); 'Practical Procedures in Clinical Medicine', (3rd edition) and he has written extensively on endocrine, metabolic and cardiac diseases.*

# The Student Syndrome

I'd spent the day in bed and, despite a restless night, the alarm clock woke me. The headache was worse than ever. My whole head throbbed. Quickly I closed my eyes against the sunlight shining through the bedroom window. I'd got photophobia. I lay back, put my hands behind my head and gently raised it off the pillow. My neck hurt: I had nuchal rigidity. Even to a medical student doing his second week of clinical studies, the diagnosis was obvious. A throbbing headache for 24-hours, dislike of light, and stiffness of the neck could mean only one thing - meningitis. With half-closed eyes I found the thermometer in the bathroom cupboard, popped it under my tongue and sat waiting on the edge of the bed - 102.4°F. I thought back - today was Friday and it was on Monday that we'd been shown in Casualty a child with meningococcal meningitis with a florid purpuric rash. I took off my pyjama jacket and inspected my arms and trunk. No rash that I could see, but nevertheless it must be meningitis.

What to do? In 1939 there was no student health service nor, of course, any National Health Service. I took two more aspirin and contemplated. Obviously I was too ill to take myself from my flat in South Kensington to St. Thomas's Hospital. Somebody would have to come and see me. But who? I didn't really know any of the registrars or lecturers who'd been teaching us during our first fortnight as clinical students. Anyway they saw only patients in the hospital. I knew only one consultant by name - Sir Maurice Cassidy, the senior physician and a cardiologist.

In desperation I telephoned Sir Maurice's secretary in Montagu Square. She couldn't have been more understanding. Sir Maurice would come and see me at about half-past-five, she said. I spent the day in bed watching the thermometer rise to 103°F. From five o'clock onwards I stood at the bedroom window looking down on Emperor's

Gate below. At five-thirty exactly a Daimler drew up at the pavement. A few seconds later the entry-phone rang. I explained that I was on the top floor. Sir Maurice was somewhat short of breath from climbing 84 steps when I met him at my front door. He was most courteous. I lay on the bed and related my history. I told him about the child I'd seen with meningococcal meningitis. He examined me from head to toe.

When he'd finished, he sat on the edge of the bed. "Young man", he said, "you haven't got meningitis. You've got 'flu. Stay in bed and go on taking aspirin. You'll be better in a couple of days. Report to my secretary tomorrow how you're getting on. Now stay here; I'll let myself out."

What a humbling and educational experience that was. I've tried to follow Sir Maurice's example all my professional life. Even more revealing was that four years later I became Sir Maurice's house-physician and subsequently his registrar. Many years later when I was responsible for the students' health service, it came as no surprise that many medical students when they felt a gland in their neck thought they'd got some potentially fatal condition, usually Hodgkin's disease.

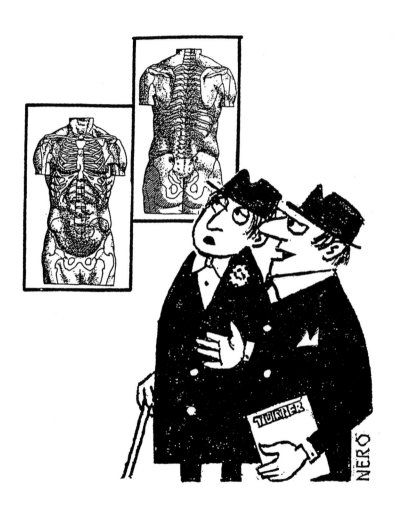

It's not by - it's Damien Hirst himself!

# Sir James Beament

*Physiologist and musician MA, ScD Cambridge, PhD London. Published many research papers and edited scientific books and journals. Elected Fellow of the Royal Society 1964. Fellow, Tutor and latterly Vice-President of Queens' College Cambridge, now Life Fellow, Professor and Head of the Department of Applied Biology, Cambridge 1969-89. Knighted 1982 when Chairman of the Natural Environment Research Council. Composer of revues, orchestral works and large-scale cantatas for chorus and orchestra performed in Cambridge, and chamber music. First performance of String Sextet Opus 50 by Royal Liverpool Philharmonic Chamber Players April 2000. Author of The Violin Explained OUP 1997 and How We Hear Music, to be published this year. Hobbies: playing jazz, the double bass seriously (alas no longer) and DIY. Married to Juliet Barker, a distinguished violin maker and teacher.*

# The Overlong Overture

In the early 1950's, amateur dramatics really were amateur, and enormous fun. In Queens' College we had the wonderful Cloister Court in which every year we performed open-air Shakespeare in front of the timbered Tudor Lodge, the envy of every Cambridge college. But there was also a room we used as a theatre; it had a minute stage and we had managed to obtain some second-hand curtains. You can tell its size because when later it had to have a license, its official audience capacity was 64 including two stewards, which really spelt the end. We used to pack 120 in there and the atmosphere for revues was really intimate! Our great achievement was a home-made switchboard and on this First Night in February our particular pride was that during the day, the students had modified the permanent wiring and could actually dim the auditorium lights.

I'd written the musical numbers for the review and began to play the overture on the piano. The house lights dimmed and the stage lights came up - that was obvious through the holes in the curtains. Then suddenly the place was plunged into darkness; I couldn't see black note from white. An urgent voice from behind the curtains near me whispered "The fuse has gone. Keep playing." And I did, for what seemed two minutes but was probably less than one, when an even more urgent voice whispered "It isn't the fuse. The fuse box has disintegrated. Keep playing." So I did. and to my enormous relief after what was officially timed as eleven minutes but seemed like half an hour, the lights came up behind the curtains again and the show started.

In the Interval I went back-stage to get the full story. In ten minutes they had got the cable used for lighting the open-air play, connected it to the remains of the fuse box, run it across the Court, broken the seals on the main electricity intake box and clipped it straight onto the live

buss-bars. The theatre tradition is that the show must go on, and it did
- virtually without a fuse between the lights and the sub-station.
The ingenuity of those student electricians was wonderful, compared
with which improvising an eleven-minute overture in complete
darkness was a mere bagatelle. The present generation have a superbly
equipped theatre. But they'll never have memories like that.

## The Magic White Powder

I graduated in the middle of World War II, and was directed to the
London School of Tropical Medicine to work on disease-carrying
insects and, in particular, lice. In World War I millions of people died
from typhus, transmitted by the louse. The only insecticides we had
were derris and pyrethrum which came from overseas. My task was to
discover why so many possible insecticides would not go through
insect skin. And then there appeared a magic white powder. Rumour
was it was smuggled in from Switzerland. It was lethal to insects
in minute amounts. It didn't appear to affect people. Could it be used
against the louse?

But lice will only feed on humans and we needed a huge supply for
testing. There was only one answer. We had to feed them on ourselves.
About a hundred were put in a little aluminium tin with a gauze through
which they could pierce our skin and suck blood. They needed to feed
for 16 hours a day. So they went everywhere with us: ten boxes in a
rather inefficient stocking, one day on one leg, one day on the other.
They were always falling out when one ran for a train. And I shall never
forget discovering at a No. 73 bus stop that half of them had

disappeared while I was at a concert in the Royal Albert Hall. Luckily they were traced back to the School, for it could have caused a germ warfare scare. Nor surprisingly, it was difficult to keep a girlfriend too.

Our field trials were simple. We 'obtained' elderly vagrants from under Hungerford Bridge, gave them a meal and an army shirt impregnated with the powder, and collected them again a week later. They were happy. All their lice were dead - and they could keep the shirt. In the winter of 1944, typhus erupted in Naples. And as the official Report said 'we rounded up the entire population and blew the dust down the collars and up the trouser legs of the males, and the females 'mutatis mutandis'. It was the first time in history that a typhus epidemic was crushed. The magic white powder was of course DDT. And my legacy of the war is a remarkable collection of skin allergies. Fortunately, the chance of my being bitten by a louse these days is small.

# Sir Alec Bedser

*Sir Alec Bedser CBE is the younger twin son of Arthur Bedser and Florence Beatrice, nee Badcock. He was educated at Monument Hill Seedy School, Woking. He served in the RAF from 1939 to 1946 and was in France with BEF 1939-40 and*

Eric and Alec Bedser

*evacuated South of Dunkirk in 1940. He became a Flight Sergeant who also served in North Africa, Sicily, Greece, Italy and Austria between 1942-46. He played cricket for Surrey CCC from 1946 to 1960 (Surrey were County Championship winners for 7 consecutive years, 1952-59). He played at Lords for England v India in the First Test after the war in 1946 making a record test debut, taking 22 wickets in his first two matches. Altogether, he played in a total of 51 test matches (21 against Australia) taking 236 wickets.*

*He was a member of the England Test Team Selection Panel from 1962 to 1985 (Chairman 1969-82); of the MCC Committee from 1982-85; of the Surrey CCC Committee from 1961 (to date) serving as Vice-President, then President in 1987-88. He was also the founder in 1955 of his own office equipment and supplies company (with his brother, Eric). He was made a Freeman of the City of London in 1968. He has written a number of books including "Our Cricket Story (with E A Bedser, 1951); Following On (with E.A Bedser, 1954); Cricket Choice (1981), Twin Ambitions (autobiography, 1986).*

## Hair We Go Again

On our first visit to Australia in 1946 we were in Sydney and we both needed a hair cut - so I found a barber and had my hair cut and subsequently Eric went to the same barber and he looked up and said "Crikey mate, I have just cut your **** hair". A true story.

# Ian Beer

*Ian Beer, CBE, is presently Chairman of the Independent Schools Council and the Council of the Winston Churchill Memorial Trust.*

*Scholar of Whitgift School and Exhibitioner of St Catherine's College, Cambridge. Second Lieutenant Royal Fusiliers during National Service and then taught at Marlborough College, Wiltshire 1955-61 as sixth form teacher and Housemaster. Headmaster, Ellesmere College, 1961-69, Lancing College, 1969-1981 and Harrow School, 1981-1991. Chairman, Academic Policy for Headmasters' Conference and then Chairman, Headmaster's Conference, 1980. Chairman Working Group for Physical Education in the National Curriculum, 1990-91. Walter Page Scholar and Evelyn Wrench Lecturer, English Speaking Union.*

*Honorary Fellow of the College of Praeceptors, Honorary Life Member of the Incorporated Association of Preparatory Schools and of the Headmasters' Conference. Awarded CBE for services to education.*

*Justice of the Peace for Shropshire, West Sussex, Middlesex and Gloucestershire.*

*Played rugby football for Old Whitgiftians, Cambridge University (Captain 1994), Harlequins, Bath and England. Chairman of Coaching Committee for the RFU and President Rugby Football Union, 1993-94. Founded SPIRE, a charity to support disabled ex-rugby players.*

# Two Headmagisterial Experiences...

As Headmaster I used to ask all pupils to make something in their spare time, using school facilities, during their first term. Going round the workshops one week-end I found a boy making a fine wooden bowl. Much impressed, I asked him what wood he was using. He did not know, so I told him that all good craftsmen would want to know about the wood they were handling and should find out. I turned away. He called me back; "I don't know what the wood is but I do know that it died of Dutch Elm disease!"

Talking to a group of boys in the Housemaster's drawing room after a house music concert I asked a fourteen year old what was bad about the school. "Nothing is bad about it, Sir." Slightly irritated, and wanting some constructive criticism, I pressed him further... "Come on", I said, "something must be bad, it cannot all be good". "No, Sir", he said "I cannot think of anything". Even more irritated I said "Well, what is the worst thing that has happened to you then?" He thought for a moment - "Well, Sir, if you really want to know it is having to talk to you now!"

# John C Benjamin

*John Benjamin served a four-year apprenticeship at Cameo Corner, the Bloomsbury antique jewellers specialising in rare and historic jewellery from Ancient Rome to the 19th Century. In 1976 he joined Phillips Fine Art Auctioneers as a cataloguer and valuer, and subsequently became International Director of Jewellery, responsible for the auction programmes in London and Geneva. In 1999 he left Phillips to set up on his own as an independent jewellery consultant.*

*A lecturer, writer and broadcaster, he has lectured extensively to professional groups, universities and societies in Britain, Europe and America, and regularly appears on BBC Television's Antiques Roadshow. He is a fellow of the Gemmological Association, holds the Association's Gem Diamond Diploma with distinction and is Consultant to the Committee of the National Association of Goldsmiths' Registered Valuers Scheme.*

# Dèja-Vu

I am a jewellery historian and part of my job involves writing and giving lectures on the subject. I also used to work in a London auction house where I was responsible for valuing and cataloguing the various properties of jewellery brought in by members of the public.

Some years ago, I was asked by a branch colleague to have a look at an interesting consignment which had been left for valuation. Housed in an old shoe box and separated by layers of yellowing cotton wool, the property comprised some fifty items of gold, silver and gem set jewellery representing the remaining stock designed and manufactured by the owner's father. My own reaction was one of amazement as I had never seen such a beautiful and comprehensive array of intricate and striking pendants, rings, necklaces and brooches. Each piece epitomised the very pinnacle of the goldsmith's art, deftly interweaving bright polychrome enamels with rare and magical gemstones such as tourmaline, chalcedony and star sapphire; a veritable treasure chest of early 20th Century British jewellery design.

It transpired that the owner still retained a large quantity of her father's papers, watercolour sketches and even many of the original workshop tools and was happy for me to research the records with a view to writing an article for an antiques magazine. In due course, I arranged for all the principal items to be photographed and prepared the ground for a lecture, which I duly delivered to several professional groups and societies. As time wore on, I also became extremely friendly with the owner and her family.

You can therefore appreciate my shock and consternation when, a year or so later, I was told that the box of jewellery had been stolen in a burglary at the owner's house. In spite of nationwide appeals in art loss magazines, jewellery journals and exhaustive police enquiries, this lovely and unique collection had well and truly vanished - a tragedy for the family and for the art world in general. All that remained was my group of colour slides, a rather bitter reminder of the real thing.

One Friday morning about six months later, I was sitting at my office desk sorting through the slides as I was giving a talk that very evening to a jewellery historians seminar. A customer rang the bell at the counter and I went to see her. After having a small group of Victoriana described and assessed, she brought out another tin box almost as an afterthought. Inside the box, unwrapped and placed haphazardly, lay the stolen jewels!

Needless to say, the Police were called and the jewellery was duly returned to its rightful owner with much rejoicing.

I often wonder at the bizarre series of coincidences which led to me, of all people, recovering the property - surely a case of intervention from above.

Toccata or no toccata there's hell of a fugue in here!

# The Rt. Hon. Tony Benn

*Tony Benn has been a Labour MP for Chesterfield since 1984 and has been elected to the House of Commons sixteen times since 1950. Previously, he was a Labour MP for Bristol South East 1950-60 and 1963-83. He was disqualified in 1960 on the death of his father, Lord Stansgate but was re-elected in August 1963 after successfully fighting peerage law and renouncing his title.*

*He was elected to the Labour Party's National Executive Committee in 1954 on which he served until 1994. He was the Chairman of the Labour Party 1971-72.*

*He has been a Cabinet Minister in every Labour Government since 1964: Postmaster General 1964-66; Minister of Technology (and Power) 1966-70; Secretary of State for Industry 1974-75; Secretary of State for Energy 1975-79; President of the Council of Energy Ministers of the EEC 1977.*

*He is the author of many books including "Arguments for Democracy"; "Parliament, People and Power"; "Out of the Wilderness - Diaries 1963-67"; "Years of Hope - Diaries 1940-62" (and audio tape); "Office Without Power - Diaries 1968-72"; "Against The Tide - Diaries 1973-76"; "Conflicts of Interest - Diaries 1977-80"; "The End of an Era - Diaries 1980-90"; "Common Sense" (with Andrew Hood). His videos include: "Speaking up in Parliament 1993"; "Westminster behind Closed Doors; "New Labour in Parliament"; "Tony Benn Speaks."*

*He was married for 50 years to Caroline Benn who sadly died of breast cancer in November 2000.*

*They have four children and many grandchildren.*

# The Boat Race

There was once a boat race between a Japanese crew and an NHS team. Both practised long and hard to reach their peak performance, but on the big day the Japanese won by a mile.

The NHS team became discouraged and morale sagged. Senior Managers decided that the reason for the crushing defeat must be found and set up a working party to investigate the problem and recommend action.

They concluded that the Japanese had eight people rowing and one steering while the NHS team had eight steering to one rowing. It immediately hired a consultancy firm to look at the team's structure. Millions of pounds and several months later, the consultants reported that too many people were steering and not enough rowing.

To avoid losing again, the team structure was changed to give three assistant steering managers, three steering managers and a director of steering services. A performance and appraisal system was set up to give the person rowing the boat more incentive to work harder.

The Japanese were challenged to another race - and won by two miles. NHS managers responded by laying off the rower for poor performance and cancelling orders for a new boat. The money saved was used to finance higher-than-average pay awards for the steering group.

# Sir Douglas Black

*Sir Douglas Black was born in Shetland and brought up in Forfarshire. He graduated in Medicine at St Andrews in 1936. Clinical training, 1936-1945 in Dundee, Oxford, Cambridge and Poona (RAMC). Research on body fluid, renal function and sprue. He was appointed Lecturer in the Department of Medicine, Manchester University, 1946, and Consultant Physician, Manchester Royal Infirmary, Professor, 1959-1977.*

*Practised general medicine and nephrology, and continued on renal disease. Wrote a textbook, "The Essentials of Body Fluid", and edited a textbook on "Renal Disease". Served on the Medical Research Council 1966-70 and 1971-77; "Chief Scientist" in the DHSS, on secondment, 1973-77.*

*Elected President of the Royal College of Physicians of London in 1977. Publication of the "Black Report" on inequalities in health, related to social class, 1980. Retired from the College in 1983, and became President of the BMA, and later Chairman of the BMA Board of Science for three years. Wrote by invitation in the Memoir Club Series, published by the British Medical Journal, an informal autobiography, "Recollections and Reflections" (1987).*

*Married Mollie Thorn, 1948. Children - Andrew, Alison and Teresa. Interests: Reading, writing, travel and listening to music.*

# Arches of Learning

When I was in the business of making after-dinner speeches, I never told stories as such; for the things that happen in real life are much stranger, and I also tended to forget the punch-line. When, as often happened, I had to illustrate the point that what one can do may depend on available resources, I recalled a wartime experience in Bengal. Strolling by one of those square ponds known as "tanks", I saw one Bengali giving a friend or patient an intravenous injection. With the arrogance of the true sahib (and in uniform as well), I asked him what he was doing (not, fortunately, what he thought he was doing). He said, "Sir, I am giving him calcium". Pursuing the matter, I asked, "Why are you giving him calcium?". I received the conclusive answer, "Calcium is what I have got".

Another experience seems funnier now than it did at the time. One foggy morning, on my way to spend a couple of days in London, I drove to Wilmslow, and left the car with the lights on, there being in those days no warning whistles. Not surprisingly, when I got back next day, the battery was flat. When I got to a garage, I found I hadn't enough money to satisfy even a reasonable demand, let alone what they asked of me. Next stop, the bank, where I was naturally asked to give some proof of identity. In doing so, I made the discovery that my driving licence was some months out of date. I didn't know at the time, but I did discover what to do - send the licence with a cheque, and it will be (or perhaps was - things may have tightened) renewed from the date of application. By contrast, when at another time I forgot to renew my car licence, I was charged back to the time when it should have been renewed. All experience is an arch of learning, as Tennyson didn't quite say; but what I learnt from those experiences was that I was qualified to be a real Professor.

# Harry "Nero" Blacker

*Harry Blacker, cartoonist and commercial artist left school at the age of fourteen. He took an apprenticeship as a process engraver but neither as a teenager nor in old age was he separated for long from his pencil and pad. His war service as a Sergeant in the Royal Artillery was only a brief sojourn. From time to time, he was invited to substitute a gun for a drawing board to produce posters for the War Office. On demobilisation, he was invited to work for Notley, one of the leading advertising*  *agencies and worked on all its campaigns for BP, the Post Office, London Transport and for Accles & Pollock, an engineering firm.*

*Blacker was never tempted away from Notleys. In his spare time, he started drawing cartoons in a style marked by straight lines and sharp angles. Under the pseudonym, "Nero", he sold his drawings to Punch, Picture Post, Lilliput and The Bystander, all leading magazines of the day. It was after his retirement at the age of sixty that cartoons became his main focus. He entered a competition for the Jewish Chronicle, won it and began a second career as the in-house cartoonist of Anglo-Jewry. In his eighties, he started his third career as a broadcaster on Radio London, Art Critic and recorder of the world of the Jewish East End. He wrote two books about it - "East Endings" and "Just Like It Was: Memoirs of the Mittel East".*

Of course I didn't walk through the streets
with this chamber pot, Doctor. I took a bus!

# Rabbi Lionel Blue

*Rabbi Lionel Blue, OBE, was born in the East End of London and educated at about 15 schools. He studied History at Balliol College, Oxford and Semitics at University College London and at the Leo Baeck College where he now teaches Prayer and Comparative Religion and where he was ordained.*

*He has published about a dozen books ranging from Theology and Prayer to Cookery, Humour and Travel. He is best known for his radio and TV religious broadcasts.*

# Drinking

When I was evacuated during the war, I used to march against the Demon Drink. I sang lustily that "My drink is water bright" and "Hurrah for the pump hurrah, her blessings are pure and free". I've forgotten the other words but at the end I used to shout out "And she is the dame for me". When I came back to London, I sang these songs to my grandfather, who listened to them gravely, and then cuffed me because he took them as a personal affront.

I don't get drunk, because I have always associated drink with religious festivals and social gatherings, and also because I fall asleep before anything can happen. I have met people who do, and it is saddening to watch the change of character it produces.

I like to hot up my tea with rum and my coffee with whisky, but if I had to choose between beverages, I would plump for that childhood delight - Liquid Bedroom Bananas.

*Ingredients*
1 pint chilled milk
2 ripe bananas
2 scoops vanilla ice cream
1 tablespoon castor sugar (or to taste)
teaspoon of vanilla
grating of nutmeg

# Dr John Burton

*John Burton was a medical officer with the Fleet Air Arm.
His experience of operating a heart-lung pump in the early
years of heart surgery led him to become a barrister on the
Western Circuit and then a Coroner in West London for 32
years until his recent retirement.*

# A Case of Mistaken Identity

The Marchioness sank after a collision in the middle of the Thames, in the middle of the night and in the middle of the shipping lane for very large ships. For the inquest, the jury and lawyers decided that they must go on the river at night to study the scene. The tide had to be starting to flood - to give the large ship involved sufficient water to float, but not be so high that it would not allow the vessel under the bridges.

The only night that fulfilled these requirements was very dark, cold and it was raining heavily. The jurors and lawyers were to be picked up at Hammersmith Town Hall by coach, and then travel to the boat that was waiting down the river. They all stood outside the Town Hall in the dark and steadily became soaked, but no coach arrived. They were all prepared for the trip. Some had dripping anoraks, some sodden clothing, wet woolly hats, plastic hoods and a variety of waterproof footwear.

Somebody suggested that they could see a light on in the Town Hall and there seemed to be somebody there. Perhaps we could wait inside away from the rain. We all trooped into the foyer and dripped on the floor. The Duty Officer rose from her desk - went white - and said "Oh My God:" "Are you ALL homeless?".

# Canon Anthony Caesar

*Anthony Caesar, CVO, FRCO, was a chorister of Winchester Cathedral, a Music Scholar of Cranleigh School and later of Magdalene College Cambridge, where he graduated in Music and History after service in the RAF.*

*He was Assistant Music Master at Eton College and then Precentor (Director of Music) of Radley College.*

*Since his ordination in 1961 his ministry has included being Chaplain of the Royal School of Church Music, resident priest at St Stephen's Bournemouth, Precentor, Sacrist and Canon Residentiary of Winchester Cathedral and Sub-Dean of H.M. Chapels Royal.*

# Extracts from a Personal Common-place Book

### The 1850's in Lydford
On Christmas Day the Curate went to the church for the celebration of Holy Communion and found the altar covered with snow that had blown in through the battered East window...

"I'll sweep it off" said the Clerk.

"On no account. God has spread his table" said the Curate; and he celebrated on the white sheet of snow.

*Sabine Baring-Gould: Book of Dartmoor*

### In the Churchyard
Here lies in horizontal position the outside case of George Routleigh, watch-maker. He departed this life Novr 14 1802, aged 57, wound up in hopes of being taken in hand by his Maker, and of being thoroughly cleaned, repaired and set agoing in the World to come.

*Epitaph on a tomb slab - Lydford*

### Faith of a Child
I like God cos he gives us food and likes me to. We and God don't like the Devil, bees and wasps.

*anon*

### Sunday Evensong at Bampton, Oxon
*Enquiry:* Were there many people in the choir for Evensong?
*Organist:* A man, a boy and a wasp.

### Good Advice
Give me the benefit of your convictions, if you have any. Keep your doubts to yourself; I have enough of my own.

*Goethe*

### Comfort Upon the Death of a Young Person
Some people are bound to die young. By dying young, a person stays that way for ever in people's memory. If he burns brightly before he dies, his light shines for all time.

*Solzhenitzyn*

## Odours

Hartley (son of Samuel Taylor) Coleridge, standing before the fire in Exeter commonroom and soliloquising in an oracular, rhapsodical and slightly affected way: "I have often thought that dogs have a language of smells, and what to us is a very nasty stink may to them be a beautiful poem."

*William Sewell, founder of Radley College,*
*quoted in Founder's Faith, compiled by Lionel James*

## A Musical Gem from a Great Performer

A great piece of music is always better than it can be played.

*Arthur Schnabel*

## Consolation

Let's not mourn when loved ones depart but rather be thankful that they were born.

*Clifford Bax to Paddy Hadley on the death of his mother*

## The Other Sullivan

His Church music was "a chronicle of sanctimonious tedium punctuated by passages of deplorable vulgarity".

*The opinion of several writers, quoted in*
*Borrowings in English Church Music by Judith Blezzard*

## Plus ça change? (1)

At the time of Edward King's accession to the See of Lincoln (1885) he was advised that the clergy of the Church of England in general and of the Diocese of Lincoln in particular could be exhaustively divided into three categories:-

Those who were going out of their minds;

Those who had gone out of their minds, and

Those who had no minds out of which to go.

## Plus ça change? (2)

The second reason why MPs now speak for so long is that padding takes longer than substance. To adapt a remark John Major once made about Neil Kinnock, their difficulty in bringing their remarks to any kind of conclusion is that, having nothing to say, they have no way of knowing when they have said it.

*Matthew Parris, The Times 4 March 1999*

## Coda

He is pretentious, has nothing to say and can't even say that.

*Benjamin Britten about another composer in a letter, January 1940*

## The Garden of Eden

O Lord, grant that it may rain every day, say from about midnight until 3 o'clock in the morning, but you see, it must be gentle and warm so that it can soak in; grant that at the same time it would not rain on Campion, Alyssum, Helianthemum, Lavender and other things which in your infinite wisdom you know are drought-loving plants.

And grant that the sun may shine the whole day long, but not everywhere (not, for instance, on Spiraea, or on Gentian, Plantain Lily and Rhodedendron) and not too much.

For so it was in the Garden of Eden; otherwise things would not have grown in it as well as they did; how could they?

*found in Plemstall Church, Cheshire*

## Empty Churches

We complain about our half-empty churches, but we need not fear, for, if the gospel of Christ were fully preached in them, they would be emptier still.

*Dean Inge*

# Sir Hugh Carless

*Hugh Michael Carless, CMG. Retired ambassador of Welsh descent on his mother's side. His great, great grandfather David Roberts, was a surgeon and farmer at Bodedern in Anglesey. A Calvinistic Methodist, he sponsored the work of Welsh missionaries overseas. But neither his practice nor the farm could support his five sons who emigrated to England. One of them did well in medicine, helped to invent Bengers Food and was knighted Sir William Roberts.*  *On his father's side, his great uncle Albert Carless, a Professor of Surgery co-published in 1898 with William Rose their "Manual of Surgery" which became an international success and ran to nineteen revised editions, the last appearing in 1960.*

*In 1942, won a bursary to study Persian at the School of Oriental and African Studies. Enlisted in army in 1943, commissioned Intelligence Corps, 1944. Also served with Royal Scots Fusiliers in northwest Europe campaign 1945. Studied history at Cambridge, joined Foreign later Diplomatic Service in 1950. Served in Foreign Office, Afghanistan, Iran, Europe and Latin America, lastly as Ambassador to Venezuela. Executive Vice-President Hinduja Foundation, 1986 to 1997. Married to painter, Rosa Maria Frontini and has two sons.*

# The Luck of the Welsh

Have you ever attended an Eisteddfod? Well, many people have. But few have ever attended an Eisteddfod in Patagonia. That is where I heard how unlucky Welshmen can sometimes be from the leader of a thirty strong Welsh male voice choir.

In the 1860s, some Welsh nationalists sailed to colonise a region of Patagonia which now forms part of the Argentine province of Chubut. By bad luck, it proved to be barren and inhospitable. The first arrivals suffered near starvation in the semi-desert environment. However, most survived and their descendants have, ever since, imparted a certain Welshness to this distant province. They even bravely hold an Eisteddfod at Trelew, the main town.

In 1977, they invited me as the then British representative in Buenos Aires. I flew south together with the male voice choir which had come out from Wales. Patagonia eventually appeared as a desolate and windswept pebble plain. The leader of the choir exclaimed that the Welsh had always been unlucky and, being a born entertainer, told this story to prove it.

*"A young man was travelling through the hills. Caught by a storm, he lost his way in the dark. A distant light shone from a lonely farmhouse. He knocked on the door. The farmer opened it suspiciously. "Well", he asked. "Sir, I'm lost. Would you let me in to dry out?"*

*The farmer let him in cautiously. His wife laid the supper. The storm continued. So the farmer grudgingly told the stranger to join them at table. The first course was mutton. The farmer carved some for his wife, some for himself and finally some for the young man. Apple tart followed. The farmer helped his wife and helped himself but deliberately refrained from helping the stranger.*

*It was then time for bed. The storm continued. So the farmer reluctantly told the young man to come upstairs with them. As there was only one bed, he made his wife lie down on the far side while he lay in the middle between her and the stranger. Before dawn, there was a commotion outside. A fox had got among the hens. The farmer leapt up, seized his gun and ran out to shoot the rascal. As soon as he was out of the house, the wife turned to the stranger, grabbed him by the arm and hissed:*

*"Now's your chance, man. Nip down and cut yourself a slice of apple tart."*

# Professor Sir Roy Calne

*Sir Roy Calne was born in Richmond, Surrey and received his medical training at Guy's Hospital in London. From 1965 to 1988 he held the Chair of Surgery in the University of Cambridge and developed an internationally renowned kidney and liver transplant programme at Addenbrooke's Hospital. He was elected Fellow of the Royal Society in 1974 and received his knighthood in 1986.*

*A tireless pioneer in the field of transplantation, Sir Roy has used his art primarily as a means of self-expression, but in his paintings he also manages to capture the more human side of his profession and in doing so, over the years, has helped to raise public awareness of the desperate need for more organ donation and raised money for a charity he set up to research into the prevention of rejection of liver grafts in children. Exhibitions of Sir Roy's paintings have been held in more than 10 countries since 1991, including Mexico, the United States, Japan, Singapore, Thailand and Germany.*

*Although Sir Roy has drawn and painted since childhood, he became particularly interested in portraying the image of transplantation after the Scottish artist John Bellany RA had a liver transplant in his department in 1988. John Bellany made the comment that "the surgeon swaps his scalpel for a brush at the drop of a hat". Bellany and Sir Roy became friends and Bellany passed on a number of useful hints particularly regarding his wonderful use of colour. As a student, Sir Roy's love of art extended to the practical illustration of science projects, especially biology. As a surgeon his interest in painting continued and in retirement he is painting as prolifically as ever.*

# Alibi for a Dye

After a few months settling in with the Gurkhas, I was suddenly issued with a posting to Japan, again out of the blue. I had mixed feelings about going to Japan, not just because of the war, but also because I was so content with the Gurkhas. The night before my departure, my friends at 33rd General Hospital threw a party for me, which was noisy, enjoyable and somewhat rebellious. Afterwards I drove back in my ancient Sunbeam Alpine to the New Territories. On the outskirts of the city of Kowloon, I was stopped by a policeman, who wasn't interested in how much I had had to drink, but wondered if I could give him a lift to his village which was next to our camp. I was happy to do so and in my open car the two of us enjoyed the fresh air of the Hong Kong night. The next day I bade farewell to my friends in the 2nd Gurkhas and was driven by jeep to a troop ship in Hong Kong harbour, bound for Japan. I was musing over this latest trick of fate, shortly before the ship was due to sail, when there was a loud commotion in the corridor. Two MPs burst into my stateroom followed by a colonel, who informed me that I was under arrest. The charge was quite clear: I was being arrested for painting a statue of the Virgin Mary outside 33rd General Hospital with gentian violet dye.

Apparently a fairly extensive paint job had been done and nobody was clear as to how the offending pigment could be removed. I was marched before the senior Colonel of the RAMC who explained the details of the charge. My simple statement that I knew nothing about the painting and that I wasn't even aware that the statue existed, was received with disbelief by the Colonel. However, I suddenly remembered the policeman I had given a lift on the outskirts of Kowloon, and the fact that the painting had taken place several hours after I had left. The Colonel permitted the Military Police to make a search for the policeman. He was easily found since I knew where he lived and he testified confirming the times that I picked him up and when I left him, so establishing my innocence. By this time my ship was well on its way to Japan, necessitating my re-posting back to my Gurkha regiment, much to my joy. Two weeks later Patsy, my future wife, arrived in Hong Kong, so that bizarre false accusation was a marvellous stroke of fate. And the true culprit? Much later, a pathology technician informed me - at top decibel from the porthole of a retreating troop ship - that his was the offending hand.

# The Very Reverend Christopher R. Campling

*Christopher Campling was born in Brisbane. After six months his family returned to England, and his father's was the first London church to be destroyed in the Blitz. Christopher was buried under a sofa. He went to Lancing College, and at the age of 18 joined the Navy, serving as a coder in a Greek Destroyer and then as a cypher officer in H.M.S. Nelson. After the war he read theology at St. Edmund Hall, Oxford, and was ordained to the parish of Basingstoke. He became Chaplain of The King's School, Ely; then Lancing College; Vicar of Pershore; Archdeacon of Dudley, Director of Religious Education and Vicar of St. Augustine's, Droitwich. In 1984 he was appointed Dean of Ripon Cathedral and retired in 1995. He had been a member of the General Synod for twenty-two years, championing liberal causes such as unity with the Methodists and the ordination of women. He was Chairman of the Open Synod Group and in 1988 was appointed Chairman of the Council for the Care of Churches. He has written a course of books for R.E. teaching 'The Way, The Truth and The Life'; Words for Worship; The Fourth Lesson; and The Food of Love: Reflections on Music and Faith, published by SCM.*

*Christopher Campling is married to Juliet. They have two daughters and a son and seven grandchildren.*

# Cyphering and Selection

In July 1945 the Third Battle Squadron was in Trincomalee making strenuous preparations for the invasion of Malaya, Operation Zipper. I was a cypher officer on the Admiral's staff aboard H.M.S. Nelson. I was also an 'ordination candidate'; and a signal came from the Chaplain of the Fleet asking that I be allowed to go to Colombo for a Selection Conference where I would be judged fit or unfit for the Church's ministry. 'Certainly not,' said Captain Biggs, the Chief of Staff. 'We are much too busy.' 'But of course he can go,' said Vice-Admiral Walker, who was a devout Anglican. We used to meet every Sunday at Holy Communion in the ship's chapel. 'But how can we get him there?' 'He can fly in my aeroplane.' So I did - and hopped over Ceylon in the Admiral's tiny aircraft, trying not to be air-sick. We spent four days shut away from the world in the Bishop's house at Colombo; and at the end of it emerged to find that the atom bombs had been dropped on Japan and that the war was all but over.

I raced to the airport, only to find that an army colonel had commandeered the Admiral's aeroplane, leaving me stranded. So I spent that day and a night with two friends hitch-hiking across Ceylon. We lit fires to ward off animals when we were stranded in the forest in the night. When I reached Trincomalee, there was the Nelson sailing away; but a signal was sent and a boat came back to pick me up, manned by two midshipmen. We sailed with the fleet to Penang, where I helped to cypher up the surrender terms.

I also went ashore with a party of communication ratings to establish a signal station, which I did by commandeering the Eastern and Oriental Hotel, which was the nearest I could find to the water-front (a story the Hotel Manager did not believe when I told him about it in 1993). We then sailed on to Singapore where Lord Louis Mountbatten joined us for the surrender itself. I was one of the three officers in the Nelson who won by draw a Japanese sword. I still own the sword; but I cannot remember ever hearing the result of the Selection Conference!

# Brigadier Conan Carey

*Educated at Belvedere College, Dublin, he enlisted in the Royal Hampshire Regiment in 1954, before attending the Royal Military Academy, Sandhurst.*

*As a subaltern and captain, he served in transportation and, as a pilot, in Army Air Corps liaison and reconnaissance units mainly in the Far East and West Germany.*

*Having qualified at Staff College, he had a number of staff and command appointments at home and abroad, becoming the Army's Deputy Director General of Transport and Movements.*

*In 1988, he left the Army to become the Director General (chief executive) of The Home Farm Trust, a national charity providing care and development services for people with learning disabilities and their carers.*

*Married, with 3 grown-up children, he now lives near Bath.*

# A Matter of Fitness

As an Army Air Corps pilot in the 1960s, I flew a variety of aircraft, one of which, the Beaver Mark 1, could be used for casualty evacuation.

In 1964, I was flying Beavers from RAF Wildenrath, near Mönchengladbach in West Germany. In July I did a casevac that led to an encounter with an ex-Luftwaffe pilot and an interesting wartime tale.

The casualty, a soldier with a back injury, had to be collected from Kristiansand in Norway, over 4 hours flying away, and brought back to the RAF Hospital, Wegberg, not far from Wildenrath. With me, I had a co-pilot and a medical orderly.

Over Schleswig Holstein, the weather was very bad and deteriorating. The prospect for crossing the Skagerrak was not good, but we did not want to turn back. A compromise was to put down somewhere and continue when the weather improved. Using a radar controlled approach, we made it to Husum, a Luftwaffe F104 fighter base, where, as a visiting oddity, we were greeted by the commander, a Colonel Asmus. Of patrician looks and bearing, he also proved to be a congenial host.

He had flown in the war as a young reconnaissance pilot - "On ze Vestern front", he had made clear during the rather liquid evening, which ensued once it was established that the weather precluded flying until the morning. He recounted how, early in the war, he had photographed RAF stations from the air and had uncovered a "secret weapon". He said "We would compare the layout of your fighter stations with ours. They were alike in almost every respect, except that the RAF's all had one extra building." At great risk, they had flown sortie after sortie to get more photographs of this mysterious building, thinking it might be crucially significant.

"And, indeed it was" he said. "It was a 'secret weapon' that gave your fighter pilots an advantage - but, we did not discover what it was for a long time and we lost aircraft trying to find out."

"And, what was it?" I asked. "It was the squash court! You see, it kept your pilots fitter and so they could take more g-forces than our Messerschmitt boys."

And, he was only half joking.

We flew on to Norway at dawn and collected our casualty. Approaching RAF Wildenrath that evening, I could see the distinctive squash court near the Officers' Mess and wondered whether it was foxing the Soviets!

Beethoven's Fifth

# Rear Admiral James Carine

*Rear Admiral James Carine is a Manxman brought up in an era when people listened avidly to ventriloquists on the wireless (radios and television were yet to come) and who said in innocent amazement "How does he do that?". Happy naïve days when the sun shone all summer long. He joined the Royal Navy aged sixteen and retired over forty years later - his most enjoyable appointment was not as an Admiral but as Commodore in command of HMS Drake over the celebration of the 400th anniversary of the Armada - a very large frog in a very small pond. Since leaving the Navy at the end of 1991, he has been General Manager of The Arab Horse Society and one of its racing stewards. His extra curricular activities include being a trustee of Combat Stress (ex-Service personnel mental welfare) and of the United Services Trustee, involved in the investment of over £44m of private regimental funds. He was also Master of a City of London Livery Company - the Worshipful Company of Chartered Secretaries and Administrators. He lives with his wife, Sally, in Wiltshire: he has four children and two Siamese cats who tolerate the humans provided they behave themselves!*

# The Wheel Goes Full Circle

In 1956, I was a young officer in HMS Superb, a large World War II cruiser, and we spent much of that year in the Gulf based in Bahrain where the Royal Navy had a shore unit, HMS Jufair. Over forty years later, I was at a World Arab Horse Breed Conference in Abu Dhabi.

The whole week had been luxurious and I took time off during an enjoyable day's visit to Sharjah to unwind by walking along the waterfront. I was looking at a fish trap made of galvanised wire mesh (in 1956 they were made of rope) when someone asked if I was American. "British" I said - Manx in truth. "I worked for the British in Bahrain" he said. He was captain of an old fishing dhow and the wheel completed full circle as he (ex HMS Jufair locally entered crewman) in a grubby dish dash and I (retired Admiral ex HMS Superb) in natty gents' suiting, squatted on his deck sipping thick sweet black coffee reminiscing about the Bahrain of 1956.

Shortly afterwards I went to Bahrain and was granted a semi-public audience by Shaikh Mohammed. I was (almost) embarrassed to monopolise the audience because, on my first visit to the island for over forty years, I think Shaikh Mohammed saw me as something of a Rip Van Winkle talking happily of the Bahrain he had known as a young man, when the capital Manama was a small town and there was virtually no industrial development.

## Favourite Silly Story

Every true Manxman crossing the Fairy Bridge on the main Castletown to Douglas road says "Good Day to the Little People". One day cycling with some other boys to watch the TT races, instead of showing due respect, I said "To hell with the Little People". Ten yards further along the road my cycle chain broke. From that day to this, whatever company I am in, I have been the most respectful Manxman the Little People have ever known.

# Dr Stuart Carne

*Stuart Carne, CBE, qualified in 1950. In 1954 he entered general practice in West London, becoming a principal 3 years later in a single handed practice in Shepherds Bush. In 1960 he merged with a neighbouring practice. In 1967 they moved into the newly built Grove Health Centre where they had enough space to work with health visitors and district nurses. In 1970 he was appointed Senior Tutor in General Practice at the Royal Post-Graduate Medical School at Hammersmith Hospital. At the same time Dr Carne became active in the (later to become Royal) College of General Practitioners and was elected to the Council in 1960. In 1963 he became Hon Assistant Secretary and, a year later in 1964 - at the age of 38 - was elected Hon Treasurer, a post he held for 17 years. From 1988 to 1991 he was President of the College, while still remaining a GP at the Grove Health Centre. In 1974 he was appointed to the Standing Medical Advisory Committee and was elected Chairman from 1982 to 1986. From his early days in medicine Dr Carne had a special interest in research. He is the author of a number of papers on various topics, mainly relating to general practice. (On 16 December 1961 he had papers published in both the Lancet and BMJ). In 1976 his monograph on child health - Paediatric Care - was published.*

*His interest in football was rewarded by his being asked in 1959 to become honorary medical officer to Queens Park Rangers FC, a job he held for 30 years.*

*He is married to Yolande and in 2001 they will be celebrating their golden wedding. They have four children and, so far, three grand-daughters.*

# Reaction to a Placebo

When I began in general practice in the 1950's placebos were an acceptable form of treatment; indeed, very few of the prescriptions in the British National Formulary at that time contained what we would now regard as active ingredients, if you excluded barbiturates, aspirin, antacids and laxatives. Part of the skill of physicians - both generalist and specialist, especially the latter - lay in devising 'elegant' prescriptions; prescribing a placebo which was different from the usual was the hallmark of the successful practitioner.

One of the advantages of placebos was that they often allowed time for the full clinical picture to emerge or for the disease - whatever it was - to get better in its own good time. Patients did not expect instant cure, but they did expect the doctor to legitimise their symptoms with a bottle of medicine; hence the comment of many of our older patients: "that was a good bottle the doctor gave me". Sometimes, too, placebos helped in keeping the more persistent symptoms away from the surgery or, quite frequently, kept the visiting list down to more manageable proportions. (In the 1950s twenty visits a day were not that exceptional, in addition to thirty or forty patients in the surgery - but that is another story for another day).

Mrs Whinger expected to be visited at least once a week, usually offering her GP the gift of a new symptom at most of these visits. She never conceded that any of my prescriptions helped her; when she no longer mentioned them it was, I suspect, because she became tired of them.

One day I asked a friendly local pharmacist (now, alas, gone to that great co-op dispensary in the sky) what might be helpful in reducing the frequency of her calls. He came up with what I thought was a brilliant suggestion: one drop (one minim, as we called it in those days) of distilled water, dispensed in an eye-drop bottle, to be taken on a lump of sugar half an hour before meals. My contribution to that prescription was to ask that the instructions on the bottle be stated precisely: 30 minutes before food (half an hour was too imprecise). As I handed the prescription to her daughter to collect from the chemist, I added that the 'medicine' would take 6 weeks to work (not your 3 weeks of the modern anti-depressants), and that I would call again after that interval.

It didn't take long for Mrs Whinger - or was it her daughter? - to trump my ace. I was on duty that night when the call came at about half past nine. "Mrs Whinger was very ill" and needed a visit. They had no phone, so the message came third hand. There was no way I could ask for details before I visited my patient. It was the middle of November; there was a 'pea-soup' fog and the roads were icy. My car skidded into a curb three times on the way there, and dented a near-side wing on the way back.

When I arrived at their flat, Mrs Whinger was sitting up in bed listening to the radio. (This was in the days before most people had a TV). "My mother can't take your new medicine." the daughter told me. "Why?" I asked. She looked at me with what I am sure was pride: "Because she's not eating!"

# Getting Our Priorities Right

The attitude of patients to illness varies enormously. The experience which sticks in my mind was with a player at Queens Park Rangers (QPR). When I was asked to be their honorary medical officer in 1959, they were a struggling third division football club. A few years later a new chairman took over and things began to look up almost immediately. 1996/67 was our big year: not only were we promoted to the second division, we also won the League Cup at Wembley against a first division side. The match which sticks in my mind during that annus mirabilis was the third round cup match which we won against another first division side. After the match one of the players came to me for advice: "I've got a sore throat, Doc". He had a roaring follicular tonsillitis and a temperature of 103°F. "Why didn't you come to see me earlier?" I asked. "What, and miss that?" was his firm reply.

# Repeat Certificates

My first three years in general practice were as an assistant - without view - in North Kensington. The surgery was in the later to become famous All Saints Road, at the wrong end of Notting Hill. Most of the patients lived in multi-occupancy, run-down, late Victorian houses. The cooking was done on a small stove on the landing. More often than not there was no bathroom. Washing was done under the tap on the same landing as the 'kitchen'. The lavatory was shared with the other residents in the house.

Mrs O'Reilly had been a patient of the practice since before the 1939-45 war. She and her husband now had five children. Two were in their teens; the other three were still too young to go to school, the war being responsible for the long interval between the second and third child. They only had two rooms. Clearly their priority for rehousing was fairly high but the Council was quite resistant to all their applications. I had recently acquired a typewriter (a novelty in London general practice in those days) and I sent a strongly worded letter to the Medical Officer of Health giving him details of the plight of that family. (Whilst speaking of Medical Officers of Health, may I send a message: "Come back, all is forgiven.")

To my amazement - and to the delight of the O'Reillys - it worked. Six months later Mrs O'Reilly came to see me, a huge smile on her face. "I've come to thank you for what you wrote to the Council" she said, "we're moving to the new town tomorrow, to a house with four bedrooms, its own bathroom - and a garden!". I wished her and her family every happiness in their new home and carried on with the rest of the 20 patients in the waiting room.

Two days later a lady came in carrying 8 medical cards. "I'm Mrs Jenkins. I've moved into Mrs O'Reilly's flat. I've come to register myself, my husband and our six children - and can I have a letter like the one you wrote for Mrs O'Reilly!"

My son wanted to be a brain surgeon but he wasn't tall enough,
so he became a gynaecologist!

# The Rt. Hon. The Lord Carrington

*Peter Alexander Rupert Carington, CH (the family name has only one 'r'), the only son of the fifth Lord Carrington, was educated at Eton and the Royal Military College, Sandhurst. He succeeded to the title on his father's death in 1938. He was commissioned into the Grenadier Guards and served throughout the Second World War, taking part in the campaign in North-Western Europe, reaching the rank of Major and being awarded the Military Cross. He resigned his commission in 1945 and took up farming.*

*Lord Carrington began to take an active part in the work of Parliament in 1946. He was an Opposition Whip in the House of Lords during the two post-war Labour Governments and when the Conservatives returned to power in 1951, he became a Parliamentary Secretary at the Ministry of Agriculture and Fisheries at the age of 32 - one of the youngest members of Government.*

*In 1956, he was appointed United Kingdom High Commissioner to Australia and then became First Lord of the Admiralty and a Privy Counsellor in 1959.*

*Lord Carrington was appointed Secretary of State for Foreign and Commonwealth Affairs following the return of the Conservatives to office after the Election in May 1979. He was Chairman of the Lancaster House Conference at the end of 1979, which led to the solution of the Rhodesian problem and the formation of the independent Republic of Zimbabwe.*

*In 1984, on relinquishing his post as Chairman of the GEC and all other business concerns, he was appointed Secretary-General of NATO. On his return to the United Kingdom in June 1988, Lord Carrington became Chairman of Christies International plc, a post which he relinquished in 1993.*

*Lord Carrington is married and has a son and two daughters. In 1988, he published his autobiography, 'Reflect on Things Past'.*

# A Cruciate Question

Some years ago, I was on board a ship in the Indian Ocean. Two days out of Singapore, a very nice lady approached me and, rather conspiratorially and in a low voice, asked me how my knee was. Rather surprised, I assured her that both my knees were in good working order. "Thank goodness", she replied, "you see, my husband took your cartilage out twenty-five years ago and he didn't want to introduce himself to you until he was quite sure the knee was in good working order!"

# Dr Carol Cooper

*Carol Cooper studied medicine at Cambridge University and the Middlesex Hospital Medical School, qualifying in 1976. After several years in hospital medicine, including a spell as senior registrar in rheumatology at Taplow, she entered General Practice and is now a part-time partner in a flourishing group practice in Chorleywood, Hertfordshire. Her articles have appeared in publications as diverse as Punch and The Lancet. Several years ago she started writing an agony aunt column for General Practitioners in BMA News Review, from which the extract adjacent is taken.*

*In addition to her regular columns, Carol is medical adviser to The Sun and broadcasts on health matters on Sky News. She is Vice-Chairman of the Medical Journalists' Association and has written several health books, mostly on parenting. A single parent, she has three teenaged boys who provide endless inspiration.*

# Dear Carol

*Need advice? Write to Dear Carol, BMA News Review, BMA House, Tavistock Square, London WC1H 9JP*

Dear Carol

I am married to a GP who has the latest mobile provided for him by his practice but refuses to switch it on. As a result, when he's on call at weekends we get dozens of calls at home while he is out. In fact people sometimes turn up on the doorstep, expecting me to dish out medical advice as well as tea, sympathy and home-made Eccles cakes. How can I make him see that occasionally I need to get hold of him when he's on the golf course?

ME, Birmingham


Dear ME

Your husband is not really living in the 20th century, is he? But then I expect the patients aren't either. As I've said before, you can't make children do something - you can only make them want to do it. Husbands are no different. So tell your beloved about a fantastic competition in which the prizes are a set of golf clubs, a week in La Manga and tickets to Augusta. There will be winners for every month of the year but the drawback is that the lucky recipients will be notified by phone as you were only allowed to put his name and mobile number down on the entry form. You can guess the rest. Hubby will have to keep his mobile switched on at all times, and furthermore everytime it rings he'll answer it immediately. Thus you will no longer have to deal with distressed or peckish patients at the door. For a touch of realism, however, you may have to buy a couple of golf balls every so often and pretend he has won a minor prize.

Dear Carol

Although I am not old, I am a care-worn GP whose hair is receding and who wears tweed jackets. People therefore think I am much older than I actually am. Patients under 40 assume I'm out of date, small children cower under the couch, and pensioners invite me to join them at bowls. I am writing to you, Carol, because I am sure that you of all people will understand my problem. So tell me, what is your own solution?

OD, Lincs

Dear OD

Basically you have three options

1. Make the most of it and retire.

2. Keep the lights switched off in your surgery - then nobody will see what you look like, although you may fall over something and do yourself a nasty injury.

3. *(Censored - Ed)*

Dear Carol

A most charming young lady patient has consulted me several times recently. One of these occasions was a home visit for a presumed chest infection. Apart from slightly heavier breathing than normal, however, her chest was clear. While I was there, she offered to show me some of her late grandfather's medical equipment. Sadly, she could not find it, and we accidentally got locked into her shed during the search. Anyway, while we were waiting for her neighbour to come to our aid, we talked about our mutual interest in music and she very kindly offered to give me flute lessons. However when I turned up this week for my first one, I discovered to my great surprise that I was meant to provide a flute for her. My girlfriend cannot believe I am this naive. What do you think I should do?

TH, Hants


Dear TH

I cannot believe you are this naive either. You should remove this patient from your list before she asks you to provide a bassoon.

*appeared in BMA News Review April 24 1999*
*reproduced with permission.*

# Dr June Crown

*June Crown, CBE, was educated at Newnham College, Cambridge, the Middlesex Hospital Medical School and the London School of Hygiene and Tropical Medicine. Her career has been in public health medicine and she has served as the Area Medical Officer in Brent and Harrow, Director of Public Health in Bloomsbury (Central London) and as Director of the South East Institute of Public Health. She was President of the Faculty of Public Health Medicine from 1995-1998.*

*Dr Crown has frequently served as special advisor to the World Health Organisation and has undertaken consultancy work related to health services reform mainly within central and eastern Europe.*

*She chaired the Department of Health review of nurse prescribing which was published in 1989 and led to the extension of prescribing rights to District Nurses and Health Visitors. More recently she has chaired the Review of Prescribing, Supply and Administration of Medicines, the report of which was published in 1999.*

*Dr Crown is Chairman of Age Concern England.*

# The X-Chromosome

I began medical training as a pre-clinical student in Cambridge. In those days, women were very much in the minority in medical schools - my year consisted of 200 men and 14 women. The clinical schools had been threatened with withdrawal of funds if they maintained their resistance to women students and were required to admit 15% women each year.

In some ways, starting at Cambridge was daunting, I was the first person in my family to be educated beyond the age of 14, so knew nothing about the ways of universities; and I came from a grammar school, while the vast majority of the class were from public schools. However, it was an enormously exciting time. The gender mix ensured a hectic school life; making friends with fellow students in my college, who were reading subjects I had hardly heard of, brought me into an intellectual environment and into spirited debates that I had never before experienced.

In spite of all this, the medical curriculum did retain my attention - I dissected, did physiological experiments, signed in to lectures, attended supervisions and wrote essays. Throughout the course, help was always at hand. The prime source of advice and support was the Director of Studies, in my case an eminent physiologist, who invariably wore a tailored jacket and skirt and a tie, and who had one of the most musical voices I have ever heard. She taught me how to frame questions, to appreciate scientific methods and to look critically at conclusions. But above all, she was, at all stages of my undergraduate career, a wonderful friend, guide and mentor.

The most memorable and valuable advice came when she was preparing us for the oral examinations. Her concern was primarily for her students, but perhaps also for the examiners - at that time an entirely male group. We were told "not to wear too much perfume, not to wear too low a neckline, and whatever you do, don't cry".

# Professor Liam Donaldson

*Liam Donaldson started his medical career in surgery and later trained in public health, holding senior posts in public health medicine and management. From the mid-1980's to the mid-1990's he was Director of Public Health for Regional Health Authorities covering the North East and Yorkshire regions of the National Health Service. From the early 1990s he combined the role of Director of Public Health with the post of Regional Director of one of the eight regional offices of the*  *National Health Service Executive. His particular experience and interests have been in strategic management and planning health policy, public health programmes, clinical governance, problems of poor professional practice and health services research. He graduated from the universities of Bristol, Birmingham and Leicester and has been awarded honorary Doctorates by the Universities of Huddersfield and Bristol. He also holds an honorary Chair of Applied Epidemiology in the University of Newcastle-upon-Tyne. He is co-author of a standard textbook of public health and has published widely on health and health service research subjects.*

*In 1998, Professor Donaldson became the 15th Chief Medical Officer for England. In this role he is the Government's senior medical adviser. He has responsibilities for policy development and implementation in improving the population's health (particularly reducing inequalities), protecting the public's health, and with the NHS leading on the implementation of clinical governance.*

# What Did You Have for Breakfast Doctor?

Up at 5.45 am, shave, shower, breakfast, a quick final skim through the facts and figures, one ear on the Today Programme - out on the street at 6.30am heading for the studios. A not untypical start to a day in the life of the Chief Medical Officer. But the day's work really begins with the sound test "We need a sound level: can you tell me what you had for breakfast this morning, doctor?".

They always say that. The first time, I though a little bit of humour wouldn't go amiss. "Two slahces of toast and a nahce cuppa tea", my Wurzel Gummidge impression used to go down big when the children were small. "Your normal voice please, doctor" came the weary voice down the headset.

Chastened, I played it straight next time. "Two slices of toast and a cup of tea." Unfortunately, that resulted in "A bit more please doctor. We haven't quite got the level." Facing the microphone I dried. I couldn't think what more to say. I had described my breakfast, for goodness sake - what more could I add? I was reduced to reciting my name and rank like a spitfire pilot captured behind enemy lines. "Two slices of toast and a cup of tea. Professor Liam Donaldson, Chief Medical Officer." If I could remember my GMC number as well, that would be the perfect length for a sound test, though perhaps not quite right as a rehearsal for coming across fluent and concerned in the actual interview.

It was beginning to get to me. When the alarm clock went off my first thought was not what should I say at the interview, but how was I going to get through the sound check.

I decided to adopt a new approach - describe the breakfast in mouth-watering detail. "Two slices of toast spread to a thickness of an eighth of an inch (3.5mm) with crushed banana and accompanied by a cup of lemon tea." No reaction from the sound engineer this time, but I could hear him thinking of words to describe a person with an obsessive personality. Breakfast, I realised can be quite eventful, if you really get involved. "Two slices of toast spread with crushed banana, a cup of tea and I could hear the man next door singing 'Nessun Dorma'" (No-one's sleeping! from Puccini's Turandot). Or another morning, "Two slices of toast spread with banana, a cup of tea and when I went out of the front door I saw a crushed Rubik Cube lying on the pavement". That last image conjured up all sorts of emotional trauma, I thought. "Thank you, doctor, we've got a level." Was there a hint of a tremor in the sound engineer's voice?

Then a week or two ago I arrived at the studio. "We need a sound level doctor. Could you tell us what you...?" "Well, I had my usual two slices of toast spread with crushed banana but we have a visitor staying with us. He was standing next to me in the kitchen and inadvertently sneezed over it. What was I to do? Eat it, so as not to embarrass him, or throw it away?" For the first time, a response: "What did you do, doctor?" As I took a breath to answer, the interview started. The levels were fine but the sound engineer was left with my moral dilemma. For all I know he may be pondering it still.

Becoming Chief Medical Officer has deepened my appreciation of breakfast, if nothing else, but I can't help worrying about the tapes. Does radio have an equivalent of those television out-take programmes hosted by Denis Norden? Some day, I fear, my crushed bananas may appear in a show called "It'll be all right in the morning". Or perhaps "The Moral Maze", with philosophical comments from the sound engineer.

My Doctor saved my life. He didn't come when I called!

# Professor Sir Christopher Frayling

*Christopher Frayling is Rector of the Royal College of Art (RCA), the only wholly postgraduate university of art and design in the world. He is also Professor of Cultural History at the RCA. Outside of the RCA, he is well-known as an historian, critic and broadcaster, with award-winning work appearing regularly on radio and television. He has published thirteen books and numerous articles on popular culture and the history of ideas, the most recent being his biography of the Italian film-maker Sergio Leone. A Trustee of the Victoria and Albert Museum, until recently a member of the Arts Council of England, and currently Chairman of the Design Council, he was in the 1980s a governor of the British Film Institute and a member of the Crafts Council.*

*Professor Frayling received a Knighthood in the January 2001 Honours List.*

# Aesthetically Acceptable

This is said to have happened at the Royal College of Art in the early 1960s; whether it did or didn't, the story has entered College folklore and says so much about art schools that I have used it to great effect on numerous occasions.

"A few years ago, an Oxford philosopher of aesthetics was invited to give a course of four lectures to our painting students at the RCA, on the subject of creativity. He arrived, armed with his immaculately prepared notes, and gave what can only be described as a very dense philosophy lecture. No pictures. There were fifty students present. At his second lecture there were twenty students, at his third five students, and at his last there was one solitary student. The eminent philosopher turned to the solitary painting student and said 'look, it's awfully good of you to come - but perhaps we'd better continue this discussion over tea or something, it seems a bit eccentric to give a lecture to one person'. To which the student replied 'I do wish you would give the lecture. I've been trying to draw you for four weeks.'"

# Mr Barry Gardiner

*Barry Gardiner is the Labour Member of Parliament for Brent North. Married with four children he was first elected in 1997. In the House of Commons Barry is respected for his work on treasury and financial matters and is a leading campaigner on Leasehold Reform where he chairs the All Party Group. Barry also founded the Labour Friends of India and is its current chair.*

# Plus ça change, plus c'est la même chose!

As a Scotsman sitting as a member for an English seat - Brent North - I have always been a keen observer of the English - so much so that I married one. My favourite parliamentary story is one which I believe goes to the very heart of the way the English see themselves.

Before Viscount Palmerston became Prime Minister he served as Foreign Secretary, in which capacity he had to meet the new French Ambassador to the Court of St James. The ambassador had heard of Lord Palmerston's haughty manner and being keen to make a good impression he began as follows.

"Monsieur Palmerston, I should like you to know that, had I not been born a Frenchman then I should have liked to have been born an Englishman." He looked up anxiously at Palmerston who replied very slowly and with great deliberation saying, "And Mister Ambassador, I should like you to know that, had I not been born an Englishman, then I should have liked to have been born an Englishman".

# Professor John Garrow

*Qualified MB ChB University of St Andrews and obtained his MD in 1957, proceeding in 1961 to MRCPE and PhD. In 1976, he was elected FRCPE and in 1988 FRCP London.*

*Member of the Scientific Staff, MRC Tropical Metabolism Research Unit, Jamaica and later Flight Lieutenant, RAF Institute of Aviation Medicine 1961-65 and Acting Director, Tropical Metabolism Research Unit, Jamaica. In 1965, he was appointed to MRC External Scientific Staff and in 1969 became Head of the Nutrition Research Group, Clinical Research Centre, Harrow, Honorary Consultant Physician, Northwick Park Hospital and Deputy Head, Division of Clinical Sciences.*

*From 1987 to 1994, he was Rank Professor of Human Nutrition, University of London, Honorary Consultant Physician at St Bartholomew's Hospital, the London Hospital and St Mark's Hospital.*

*He is the author or co-author of the following monographs: 'Electrolyte metabolism in severe infantile malnutrition.'; 'Energy balance and obesity in Man.'; 'Treat obesity seriously: a clinical manual.' He was the Editor of the European Journal of Clinical Nutrition 1988-1999.*

# Food for Thought

In my first medical year (1947) there were only 10 of us straight from school, the others were sophisticated, self-confident ex-servicemen. They had a hard time in the preclinical years because their book-learning was a bit rusty, but in the clinical course their knowledge of Life gave them a rapport with patients with which I could not compete. My niche would have to be in some laboratory. Our professor of bacteriology claimed he had often saved clinicians from diagnostic disasters, so he would serve as a role model. I saw myself running into the ward flourishing a laboratory report, gasping "Its dengue!" and all the clinicians would be very grateful.

So, when I qualified, I went to do a pathology job in Jamaica, where they had malaria, leprosy and yaws. That should provide scope for report-flourishing. I could find ring forms in thick blood films, but the year after I arrived in Jamaica WHO had a malaria eradication programme, which deprived me of my best trick. There was some leprosy (but not diagnosed by me). Yaws was microbiologically and immunologically identical with syphilis, from which it could be distinguished by clinical features.

There was quite a high mortality among children with measles, but the factor that determined their prognosis was not the infecting organism, but their nutritional state. Indeed nutrition was the hot topic. There was no plausible explanation why some malnourished children became oedematous, with massive fatty infiltration of the liver and dermatoses (kwashiorkor), while others shrivelled to skin and bone, but had no oedema or skin changes (marasmus). It happened that the leading researcher in this field (now Prof John Waterlow FRS) was then working on his own in Jamaica as MRC external staff in the physiology department, so I went and asked him for a job, and got it.

# Bruce George

*He has been a Labour Member of Parliament for Walsall South since February 1974 and Chairman of the House of Commons Defence Committee since 1997 (having been a member since the inception of the Committee in 1979). He was also the Senior Opposition Member from 1992-1997.*

*A member of the UK Delegation to the NATO Parliamentary Assembly (formerly the NAA) since 1981, he was instrumental in the expansion of the NAA to include former Warsaw Pact countries as Associates.*

*Since July 1999, Bruce George has been Vice-President of the OSCE Parliamentary Assembly. Since 1997 he has been Leader of the UK Delegation to the OSCE Parliamentary Assembly.*

*In total, he has authored or edited seven books (two of which are pending publication) and over two hundred chapters of books/conference papers/reports/articles on subjects including: UK defence and foreign policy; the Warsaw Pact; Mediterranean security; arms control and disarmament; Confidence Building Measures; terrorism; comparative defence decision-making; NATO; statutory regulation of the private security industry (an issue on which Bruce George has campaigned since 1977, including the introduction of six versions of a Private Member's Bill); crime and policing; parliamentary reform; and British Politics.*

*He is married to Lisa Toelle, formerly of St. Louis, Missouri, USA since 1992.*

*His recreations include reading and supporting Walsall Football Club.*

# Lost for Words

As a young (28 years old) Labour candidate for the unwinnable election at Southport - in the event I came a poor third - I went on a tour of the hospital conducted by the matron who reminded me a little of Hattie Jacques.

At what I hoped was the end of the tour she visited the Coronary Care Unit and with reluctance I accompanied her. I didn't wish to be seen touting for voters amongst the desperately sick five days before the election, In the corner was a very sick man with every surgical device known to man inserted in him, 'Hattie' frogmarched me over to the foot of the bed and said, "This is Mr George, he's the Labour candidate for the election on Thursday".

The poor man tried to respond but his remarks were inaudible. She pulled me halfway down the side of the bed and said, "The elections are on Thursday. Mr George has come to see you". Again a pained look and further, incomprehensible grunts that neither of us could understand. Finally she pulled me even closer to his face and medical equipment. "Actually, the real reason he's here is to ask you for your vote." At this stage I was crushingly embarrassed. He made another valiant attempt to communicate his response and both the matron and I struggled to understand. Finally, some words with great pain escaped his lips, '*"#% off!!!!".

I did!!!!

# The Rt. Hon. Sir Edward Heath

*Edward Heath was educated at Chatham House, Kent and Balliol College, Oxford (President of the Oxford Union 1939).*

*He saw active service with the Royal Artillery during the Second World War reaching the rank of Lieutenant Colonel.*

*In 1950 Sir Edward became Member of Parliament for Bexley. From 1974 he was Member of Parliament for Bexley Sidcup, and Old Bexley and Sidcup from 1983.*

*During his long and distinguished political career he has been Minister of Labour (1959-60), Lord Privy Seal (1960-63), Secretary of State for Industry, Trade and Regional Development and President of the Board of Trade (1963-64), Leader of the Opposition (1965-70), Prime Minister (1970-74), and Leader of the Opposition (1974-75). While he was Prime Minister he successfully completed the negotiations for Britain's entry into the EEC. He has been Father of the House of Commons since 1992.*

*Sir Edward is patron of many charities and voluntary organisations nationally and within Old Bexley and Sidcup. His publications include, "One Nation: A Tory Approach to Social Problems" (1950), "Travels: People and Places in My Life" (1977), and his autobiography, "The Course of My Life"(1998).*

*Sir Edward's recreational interests include sailing, music and travel.*

# American Football Anecdote

I first watched a game of American football in Carolina during a debating tour of the USA, when I saw Duquesne beat North Carolina State at Raleigh, North on Saturday 11 November 1939. I was immediately fascinated and, latterly, have become a considerable devotee of Super Bowl, the annual climax of the American football. These games can be watched not only with the naked eye or field glasses, but also on the giant TV screens placed around the arena which give the referees the opportunity of replaying in the public gaze any disputed decisions which they or their officials might have made.

I well recall one particularly controversial refereeing decision, which all the other match officials queried three times. He confirmed it twice and, each time he did so, three men in front of me rose and cheered. Then, to their horror, the referee lost his nerve and changed his mind. At this, the two men next to them leaped to their feet, overjoyed at their neighbours' reversal of fortunes. Having cut my sporting teeth on the tough terraces of Highbury, I waited for the inevitable explosion of lively partisanship. I was to be disappointed. The other three remained calm, collected - and seated. There was no ill feeling, no friction and not even a vigorous exchange of views. Never mind our football hooligans, this was a display of tolerance which would have put the House of Commons to shame!

# John Inverdale

*BBC TV and radio presenter, John Inverdale has spent most of his own personal sporting life taking mediocrity to previously unsuspected depths. However, on the eve of the World Cup Final in 1995, he achieved one of the few moments of note during 30-odd years of dropping passes, missing open goals, simple putts and straightforward volleys. In the match between the northern hemisphere media and the southern hemisphere media in Johannesburg, he arrived in the*  *changing rooms before the rest of the team and immediately selected the no. 15 jersey. Ten minutes later, the greatest player ever to wear that shirt on the international rugby field walked in. It was Serge Blanco - the legendary Frenchman. He looked around for the same shirt. John threw him another jersey. "Moi quinze vous dix," he said matter-of-factly, and so it was. Selected ahead of Blanco. One to tell the grand-children about.*

*John began his broadcasting career at BBC Radio Lincolnshire before moving to the Radio 4 "Today" programme and then to Radio 5 Live. He presented "Rugby Special" on BBC2 for many seasons and now fronts "Grandstand" on occasions, as well as the chat-show, "Onside".*

# The Rugby Shirt

As Barry Manilow might have put it - "His name was Thambo, he came from Joburg" - and he didn't like rugby. I knew that because the moment he took my bags to the hotel in Johannesburg, he said to me: "You here for the rugby? I don't like rugby."

Well South Africa was a divided country as the Rugby World Cup began in 1995. Rugby was the white man's sport. Soccer was for the blacks, and never the twain would meet. But as the weeks went by, and as the Springboks continued to improve and the possibility of them reaching the final increased, there was a general shift in the public perception of the sport. Suddenly you noticed black schoolchildren wearing the green and gold jerseys. News bulletins, whether staged or not, showed township kids throwing a few oval balls around. And then on the morning of the final, when South Africa played New Zealand, one of those moments that you never forget, occurred over the bacon and hash browns at breakfast.

Thambo and I had smiled at each other over the six weeks that we'd stayed in, truth to tell, not one of the great hotels of our time. He had one of those gleaming all-embracing smiles that make it appear as if the sun's out, even when the skies are leaden grey. We'd exchanged a few words, but little more. That morning, in slovenly mode, I was wearing a Springbok rugby shirt. He came over to our table. "Was there any chance that I might be able to give him that-shirt after the match because he was so proud of his country on that day?" "But you hate rugby", I said. "No, he didn't." He had come to love it as the weeks had gone by, and he wanted to wear his country's colours on the day of the final, but he couldn't afford to buy one of the official shirts. Much to the chagrin of those around me, I took it off there and then and gave it to him. Most of my breakfast companions were on the point of bursting into tears at the sight of a semi-naked body at 8 o'clock in the morning. Arnold Schwarzanegger it wasn't. But Thambo actually did wipe away a few tears. We embraced over tea and toast, and he promised to wear the shirt all day.

Sport as a force for good. It's a moment I've never forgotten, though I'm sure it's disappeared into oblivion for him. But I'd love to know if he's still got the shirt.

# Greville Janner, The Lord Janner of Braunstone

*Greville Ewan Janner QC, author, lecturer, journalist and broadcaster was created a Life Peer in the County of Leicestershire in 1997. He was educated at Bishops College School, Canada, St Paul's School and Trinity Hall, Cambridge. He was a Harmsworth Scholar of the Middle Temple.*

*In 1970 he was elected Member of Parliament (Labour) for Leicester North West and from 1974 to 1997 was Member of Parliament for Leicester West. He was the Founder and President of the World Executive Council against Anti-Semitism and Secretary of the All Party War Crimes Group.*

*He has published 65 books mainly on public speaking, law, presentational skills including 'Employment Letters'; 'Complete Speechmaker'; 'Complete Letter writer'; 'Communication' and 'One Hand Cannot Clap.' He is a member of the Magic Circle and a member of the International Brotherhood of Magicians.*

*He speaks 9 languages and is learning Arabic.*

# Misunderstandings

Not long ago, I was fortunate enough to travel by Richard Branson's Virgin Airline, Upper Class. They assured me that a car would pick me at the House of Lords at a fixed time.

When the time arrived, I stood with my luggage at Peers' Entrance. No car. So I telephoned the airline and they assured me that the car was waiting for me outside the House of Lords. I went back to the entrance and lo and behold, a fine limousine had drawn up outside, driven by a very well dressed young woman.

I opened the rear door and said to her: "Virgin?"

She looked me straight in the eye and said: "I beg your pardon...!"

"Are you from Virgin Airlines?" I enquired, swiftly.

After another long pause, the driver said: "My lord, the answer is no to both your questions!"

PS: The true Virgin vehicle was waiting at the other entrance, in Black Rod's Garden.

# The Rt. Hon. Lord Jenkins of Hillhead

*Roy Jenkins is Chancellor of Oxford University, President of the Royal Society of Literature and until January 1998 was Leader in the House of Lords of the Liberal Democrats. He was a founder of the Social Democratic Party and its first Leader. He is a former Chancellor of the Exchequer and Home Secretary, and a former President of the Commission of the European Communities. He was SDP Member of Parliament for Glasgow Hillhead from 1982 until June 1987.*

*Roy Harris Jenkins is the son of the late Arthur Jenkins, formerly miners' leader and Member of Parliament for Pontypool.*

*When Labour took office in October 1964, Roy Jenkins became Minister of Aviation; in December 1965 he became Secretary of State for the Home Department; in November 1967 he became Chancellor of the Exchequer.*

*At the change of government in 1970 he was elected leader of the Labour Party, but resigned from this position and from the Shadow Cabinet in 1972 in protest against the Labour Party's equivocation on the European Community issue. In November 1973 he returned to the opposition front bench. He became Home Secretary for the second time when the Labour Party returned to office in March 1974, a post which he held until September 1976. From 1977 to 1981 he was President of the Commission of the European Communities.*

*Roy Jenkins has written several books which include 'Sir Charles Dilke, a Victorian Tragedy', 'The Labour Case', 'Asquith'; a volume of Speeches and Essays; 'Afternoon on the Potomac?' based on Henry L. Stimson Lectures at Yale University, and 'What Matters Now', a series of contemporary speeches. In 1974 he published 'Nine Men of Power', a collection of biographical essays which had appeared in The Times. In 1985, 'Partnership in Principle', in 1986 'Truman, a biography of the U.S. President', and in 1987 'Baldwin, a study of the inter-war British Prime Minister'. In 1988 he published 'A Gallery of Twentieth Century Portraits', in 1989 'European Diary, 1977-81', in 1991 his autobiography, 'A Life at the Centre', in 1993 'Portraits and Miniatures', in 1995 'Gladstone' (winner of the 1995 Whitbread Biography Award), and in 1998 'The Chancellors'.*

*He was made a Fellow of the Royal Society in 1992 and an Order of Merit in 1993.*

*He is married to Dame Jennifer Jenkins, until recently Chairman of the National Trust, and has two sons and a daughter.*

# President Richard Nixon
# - 37th President of the United States

The Nixon Administration was fresh in office, and although I was far from being an admirer of that flawed President who nonetheless showed streaks of imaginative boldness before subsiding into tragedy, I was curious to inspect the new regime at home. I had already seen Nixon in operation during a bizarre day in London in late February. It was bizarre because it had exhibited a bewildering variety of Nixon's facets. It had begun with a scheduled two-hour Cabinet-room discussion between the President with a small entourage on one side and three or four senior members of the British Government on the other. Nixon opened with a half-hour informal exposé and did it brilliantly. Then coffee was brought in, and mixed up with putting or not putting sugar and milk in his cup the President mysteriously succeeded in picking up a crystal inkwell and pouring its contents over his hands, his papers and some part of the table.

Consternation broke out, particularly on the British side. It was like a Bateman cartoon, with extremes of surprise, horror and sympathy being registered. Sir Burke Trend, the Secretary of the Cabinet, even poured cream over his own trousers, although it was not clear whether this was because he was so shocked or because he thought the President would feel less embarrassed if carelessness verging on slapstick appeared to be a Downing Street habit. Blotting paper, napkins and towels were rushed in, and eventually Nixon was taken out to nailbrushes and pumice stones. They were unavailing. After a long interval he came back with his hands still stained. It was a real Lady Macbeth scene, and it completely ruined his concentration. He could do nothing but look at them for the rest of the morning. His brilliance was all gone. The discussion never regained any verve and was adjourned early. He somewhat recovered his composure over lunch.

Before his next appearance with us the resources of the travelling field laundry or whatever accompanies the President had proved adequate for at dinner he was spotless and once again on very good form. He made an excellent speech partly welcoming ex-left-wing-weekly editor John Freeman, whom Wilson had just appointed to Washington after four years as High Commissioner in Delhi, and suggesting that as Freeman became the old diplomat he (Nixon) would endeavour to be 'the new statesman'.

The festivities were rounded off by a little post-prandial charade which Wilson had organised in the Cabinet room. All members, those who had not been at dinner as well as those who had, were required to be present and perform for the benefit of the visitors, as though they were taking part in a real Cabinet. Some of us, notably Crosland and I, were I am afraid a little sullen or shy about doing our pirouettes, but we were more than made up for by Crossman and Benn, who put on bravura performances. Crossman at least struck some rather mordant political paradoxes while Benn trilled away about sputniks and Bible readings. The President took up what was perhaps the only possible polite position, looked amazed that 'two little heads could know so much', and expressed suitable admiration to the Prime Minister about the brilliance of his Cabinet.

*An Extract from, "A Life at the Centre", autobiography of the Rt. Hon. Lord Jenkins. Published by Papermac. Reproduced by kind permission of the author.*

# Dr Robert Kendell

*Dr Kendell, C.B.E. qualified from Cambridge University after clinical training at Kings College Hospital, London. He did his psychiatric training at the Maudsley Hospital and the Institute of Psychiatry. He was Professor of Psychiatry at the University of Edinburgh 1974-91. He was Dean of the Edinburgh Medical School, 1986-90 and Chief Medical Officer for Scotland 1991-96. He was elected President of the Royal College of Psychiatrists 1996-99.*

# Getting the Right Examiner

Surgical finals. The memory of my clinical examination still sends shivers down my spine forty years later.

At the time I took my finals I had just obtained my hospital's surgery prize, so I was feeling 'quietly confident' as I went into the examination hall. I had forty minutes to examine my patient, who was a thin, sallow, middle aged man, and because I didn't have time to spare I wasted no time asking him what his original symptoms had been but homed straight in on the crucial issue. Tell me about your operation I said, and he did. He had a vertical abdominal scar and described having had most of his stomach removed for an ulcer two years before (this was long before the days of beta blockers and proton pump inhibitors) and had recently been getting very uncomfortable feelings of distension after meals, sometimes accompanied by profuse sweating and once or twice by loss of consciousness. It seemed fairly clear that he had had a partial gastrectomy and vagotomy and was now getting a 'dumping syndrome'.

The only other useful information I elicited was that he smoked (most men did in those days) and also had mild diabetes for which he was taking tablets.

I thought I knew enough about the 'dumping syndrome', its causes and treatment, though I had never previously encountered the syndrome in a diabetic and realised that I might quickly get into trouble discussing the role of hypoglycaemia in this particular patient's dumping syndrome. As he was a bit anaemic and underweight I looked carefully for signs of an underlying malignancy but I could find nothing, so I could say fairly confidently that I didn't think he had a gastric cancer.

At that stage I had a few minutes left and couldn't think of anything else to do. So I started examining his central nervous system, mainly because that was the only part of the standard physical examination I had been taught that I hadn't yet done. I went methodically and rather unintelligently through his cranial nerves, I to XII, and then picked up a patella hammer. I tapped his arms in approximately the right places, scratched his abdomen four times with a pin and then turned back the blanket to examine his legs. At that point the bell rang summoning me to the examiners' table and simultaneously I saw, to my horror, that some swine had amputated both my patient's legs in mid-thigh, and the blighter had never told me!

I walked slowly towards the examiners' desk like a condemned man walking to the gallows. This was it. I was going to fail, and in surgery too. So much for dreams of a glittering career! I also began to experience symptoms rather like my patient's 'dumping syndrome' - an unpleasant epigastric sensation and a cold sweat.

Fifteen minutes later I emerged into the June sunshine knowing how a convict must feel after a last minute judicial reprieve. By great good fortune my examiner had been a specialist in gastric surgery. As soon as I had started to talk about the 'dumping syndrome', his eyes lit up and most of the next ten minutes was occupied by him explaining to me that the patient had had the wrong kind of partial gastrectomy and that if only he had had the right kind - his own invention, as it happened - he would almost certainly not now be experiencing those unpleasant symptoms. We talked a bit about the differentiation between benign and malignant gastric ulcers, but diabetes, the bilateral amputation and the fact that the poor man was probably confined to a wheelchair were never mentioned by either of us. They were clearly irrelevant to the essential surgical problem.

I don't remember his name but the faeces is familiar!

# Sir Robin Knox-Johnston

*After serving for 14 years in the Merchant Navy, Sir Robin turned to yachting and in 1968-69, became the first person to sail alone and non-stop around the world, a record-breaking voyage of 312 days. Subsequently he has participated in many ocean races, including the Whitbread and in 1994 set a new world record for the fastest circumnavigation of the world under sail. He is President of the Sail Training Association, an organisation which sends some 2000 young people to sea in its own square riggers for a taste of Tall Ships adventure, basically character development, and which also runs the annual Cutty Sark Tall Ships races.*

# A Current Event

We had been allowed a day off by the Mate to sail the ship's gig up the creeks behind Vizagapatam in India. As we approached a low road bridge, I told my two fellow apprentices that we would round up alongside it and take down the mast and then row back to our ship. I duly approached the bridge and the bowman suddenly called out that he had felt a shock. I told him rather dismissively that it was probably an electric eel touching the keel, but the next moment there was a huge flash and he was thrown four feet in the air. "Blimey" said the third apprentice, "some electric eel!". The unfortunate bowman was slumped forward and I leapt forward to check he was OK. He was badly burned about his legs but otherwise all right, but obviously needed medical attention. We beached the boat and I climbed overside in three feet of mud. The injured man was helped onto my shoulders and I carried him ashore, stopped a passing bus, and had us taken to a nearby Indian Naval base. There, covered in mud, with an injured man on my shoulders, I was confronted by an immaculate Sikh Petty Officer who kept his distance whilst dealing with my request for a Doctor. Then he marched us across a vast, sun baked parade ground to the medical centre.

The young Lieutenant Doctor who came immediately quickly started dealing with the burns and apologised for the lack of electricity. The base's supply had apparently abruptly ceased some half an hour before. The injured man started to say something about the coincidence of the timing but I placed a hand quickly over his mouth. There seemed no point in admitting that it was our forestay, catching an unnoticed overhead power supply line that had earthed through the apprentice to the water inside the boat and disconnected an entire naval base!

A true story!

# David Kossoff

*Far more educated to draw than to act. All on scholarship; no fees. "They paid me! We were so poor I qualified for every sort of grant." Top furniture designer at 19. Decided to become an actor. Parents horrified. Outbreak of war decided otherwise. Chained to drawing-board during the war as a "sort of unimportant backroom boy".*

*Every spare moment given to working in an amateur group theatre. Noticed. BBC contract waiting at war's end. Stayed six years. Left, and shot ahead. TV, films, the lot.*

*Has a British Academy Award "upstairs somewhere in a cupboard." The Meeting-the-Queen photo however is hanging up. "We both look nice in it."*

# A Cautionary Tale

The actor was having a splendid day. He had taken part in a Great Thanksgiving service in a Great Cathedral. His contribution, a reading from one of his popular books of Bible Stories, had been amusing and had raised chuckles during a rather solemn occasion, not only among those seated in the Nave but also those who were Titled and Eminent in the Quire. He had received many compliments. He had joined many Distinguished Persons at a Reception and Lunch and received more.

He had enjoyed very much both the recognition and the food and drink. A quiet-living semi-retired man in his seventies he had preened a little, been perhaps a bit gracious and "famous"; a touch smooth.

All was noted by the Almighty, who for many years had been amused by the actor's informal way with the Book. An Angel was summoned and sent to the birds who lived in the trees of the Cathedral Green, where the actor had been allowed to park his car among other privileged persons. "Those of you", said the Angel to the birds, "who have recently filled yourselves with dark fatty sticky foods will make deposits all over the Ford in the corner. Be generous. Hold nothing back!"

The actor, goodbyes made, replete, sunwarmed by his stroll across the Green, was appalled to find his car in such a state. On his way home he used a car wash, twice through, and drove on. On alighting from his car he had a further shock. The car washes had been entirely useless. He changed into less elegant clothes and set to work, with solutions, suds, scrapers (and much swearing) until the car was spotless. Of all his routine tasks this was his least liked, hated even.

He tidied all away, humility firmly back in place. He had long acquaintance with the ways of the Almighty and had no complaint.

# Sir Alexander Macara

*Educated at Irvine Royal Academy, University of Glasgow, and London School of Hygiene & Tropical Medicine.*

*Currently Honorary Visiting Professor of Health Studies in the University of York; Chairman of the National Heart Forum and of the Alcohol Research Forum of Alcohol Concern; Chairman of the Public Health Medicine Consultative Committee; an elected member of the General Medical Council and a member of the Council of the Academy of Medical Sciences. He is a governor of the London School of Hygiene & Tropical Medicine, and remains a member of the Council of the British Medical Association, of which he was Chairman from 1993-1998.*

*His extensive international experience includes work as a Consultant and Adviser on Human Resources in Health for the World Health Organisation since 1970; Secretary General of the Association of Schools of Public Health in the European Region (ASPHER) for 13 years; and the establishment of the World Federation for Education & Research in Public Health in 1988. He was President of the European Forum of Medical Associations in 1994 and is currently Chairman of its Task Force on Tobacco. He has been a member of the Committee of Doctors in the European Union since 1980.*

*He has served extensively as External Examiner and Visiting Professor at home and overseas. He has given numerous named lectures and received a number of honorary doctorates and awards in the field of Public Health.*

## A Scottish Pile

*Question:*

"Why are Scots practising medicine in England regarded by their colleagues as being like haemorrhoids?

*Answer:*

"Because if they come down but go back up again they are an irritant, but only for a time. If on the other hand they come down and stay down, they are a pain in the ****."

# Professor Sir Roddy MacSween

*Professor Sir Roddy MacSween was President of the Royal College of Pathologists from 1996 to 1999. Born in the island of Lewis, he is a native Gaelic speaker who learnt English when he went to school. A graduate from the University of Glasgow he became Professor of Pathology there in 1984 and retired in 1999. Professor MacSween had a special interest in the pathology of liver diseases and established an international reputation in this field; he is the senior editor of "Pathology of the Liver", of which a 4th edition is to be published in the summer of 2001.*

*He was Chairman of the Academy of Medical Royal Colleges from 1998-2000. He is an appointed member of the General Medical Council, representing the Royal College of Pathologists and the Royal College of Radiologists. He was knighted in June 2000 for his services to Pathology and Medicine.*

*Sir Roddy is married with two children: his wife Marjory was a Dermatologist as is his daughter Ruth, now working in Canada; his son Gordon, a graduate in production engineering is now in e-commerce. The family find relaxation in their home near the Mull of Kintyre where Sir Roddy indulges his leisure interests in golf, hill-walking, rough gardening, reading and more golf! He is a past-Captain of Dunaverty and Machrihanish Golf Clubs.*

# A Life in the Day of the President

Spontaneously wake at about 6.30 am; press my endogenous snooze button - an extra five minutes: get up and switch off alarm clock which is permanently set for 6.45: shave and dress, a quick surf of the Ceefax, make my daily tie selection (must get rid of some of the many I compulsively buy): fruit juice in the well-appointed President's flat - if only I knew what to do with the kitchen-ware. At home in Glasgow, it is so much easier; I have taken instructions from my patient wife Marjory - 'close the microwave oven door' - and there is a lovely meal when the bell goes: I experimented only once myself and burnt a salad! So, out for breakfast. First a stroll to Piccadilly to get my Telegraph: exchange a few pleasantries with the vendor - have to check my change: he does have problems with Scottish notes (especially the £2 ones). For a light breakfast - 'Marios' in Lower Regent Street; for an English breakfast, the Athenaeum and have a glance at some of the other papers - I have preformed antibodies to The Grauniad and if I look at it I run the risk of anaphylaxis.

At my desk by 7.45: marvellous views across St. James's Park to Westminster (contrasts with my Glasgow office and a view of a partially demolished and crumbling Western Infirmary). Official papers to read: try to finish some draft reports: touch base with Maureen (my Glasgow secretary) soon after 8.30 am: Julia (my London secretary) comes in at 9.30 am - works an hour later and so I have secretarial cover for nine hours a day (marvellous). They keep duplicate diaries and all engagements are double checked - I have my own: I live in terror of being double booked.

Some days entirely comprise meetings: may start at 8.30am (the then Chief Medical Officer, Sir Kenneth Calman was an early starter - it's a characteristic of the Glasgow mafia).

Julia opens the mail and checks it in: if there are no meetings this is dealt with at about 10.00 am: 20% can be dealt with right away (shorthand dictation); 20% require further attention (deliberation and a longhand draft); 20% require consultation within the College; 20% comprise consultation documents and these can weigh pounds rather than being gauged in pages - NHS (E), Government Departments, BMA; 10% are a miscellaneous bag - letters from Members and Fellows (Traumatised from Thurso who enquires whether PFI is a threat to EQA and CME or could be a surrogate for CPD; I find a personal telephone call is immediately beneficial for correspondent and President); and a final 10% which deserve their final resting place in the white round plastic filing cabinet under the desk.

I do a regular 'ward-round' most days - the examinations section, the finance section, audit, publishing, manpower, CME, academic affairs and the staff at reception: a friendly chat with those doing the real work on a day to day basis: this way I feel I better appreciate what a life in the day of the College is all about. Lunch is usually a sandwich snack at my desk, unless there is a visitor or guest whom I take to the Athenaeum. The afternoons are sometimes a less strenuous mixture of meetings, reading of papers or drafting responses to consultation papers. Newsworthy items can suddenly appear and I realise how little I like dealing with the press or the media.

Quietness in the College after 5.30 - but useful time to do re-checking or undertake final editing of consultation responses. The evening meal is not a problem - home cooking (take-away type), a light meal in one of the many eating places close to the College, a heavy meal comprising one of the numerous dinners which characterise the London medical scene (my role as the College's stomach (and liver!) is significant) - one has to be abstemious - I can recommend the thirst-quenching and appetising effects of diet tonic with ice and lemon: no potatoes if you're having the sweet: no sweet if you're having the cheese: avoid the port if you've had more than two glasses of red wine or four glasses of white and one of red - oh... confusing! Sometimes there has to be homework for the next day but there are evenings off - cinema, theatre from time to time: I've seen more plays in the last year than in the previous five.

Oh! and then there are the bad evenings - a dash to Heathrow or Gatwick to get back to Glasgow in the frozen North. I avoid the 'sleeper' if at all possible - Virgin trains are not for sleeping! Departmental and University duties have to be dealt with on some day(s) each week. These require less preparation but familiarity must not breed contempt: my senior staff in the Department contribute enormously to making my Presidential life in London possible: they still recognise me and my trainees have heard of me: it is only some of my colleagues from other University Departments I have problems with - but is it they or I who are not spending so much time in Glasgow? I keep my histological eye in by reporting a weekly round of liver biopsies (local and referred). What a chore I hear you say - no, they were never so but now they are wonderfully therapeutic and reassure me I'm still a histopathologist. Then my other wonderful therapies - a game of golf (sometimes two!) at the weekends and home cooking (I don't think Marjory really knows how to use a microwave oven either).

Time for bed - I always try to watch Newsnight and wonder whether Wark or Paxman is the better role model for a President. I sometimes wander on to the roof and admire the wonderful vista of the London skyline; the now reduced noise of the traffic acts as a mild sedative. In bed I browse through whatever novel I'm reading and this takes me past midnight (I do believe it's not good for you to go to bed the same day as that on which you got up). I sleep like a stone usually, but occasionally I have a blinding insight into and promptly think I have solved some major problem in those dreamy lucid intervals around 3 am - would I could remember these when my batteries kick in again at 6.30 am with another day in prospect.

# Professor Anthony Myles Martin

*Professor Martin graduated from St. Andrews University in 1963. Post Graduate Clinical Training Edinburgh Royal Infirmary, Glasgow Royal Infirmary. Physician and Nephrologist, Sunderland Royal Hospital. Undergraduate and Post-Graduate Teacher and Examiner who is consultant in Medical Education to the Lord Kitchener School of Medicine, Khartoum, and The Medical School, Juba, Sudan. Senior Medical Specialist to the Royal Navy on active recall (RNR) 1971-1990. Part time lecturer for the National Trust for Scotland. Wood sculptor, treevangelist, compiled "Meet the Conifer Family" for the Royal Botanic Gardens, Edinburgh.*

# Tales from the Scottish Highlands

## A Grape By Any Other Name

In the late 60's as SHO and Registrar I undertook, single handed Family Practice locums in Wester Ross, 100 miles from the nearest hospital, on the Atlantic coast surrounded by the most majestic mountains in Scotland.

The weather, the culture and the people interacted in a unique way that determined the doctor's life. It was a peaceful autumn evening that found me driving round Loch Ewe to Inverewe gardens for an evening meal with friends in the "Big House" on Am Ploc Ard. I was welcomed with a fine French wine and just beginning to mellow when a call came through. "Oh doctor, I'm sorry to trouble you but a terrible thing has happened. My husband has just come in with a grape up his nose. Can you see him as soon as possible". "Alright dear, don't worry. Bring him to the Poolewee village hall and I'll take it out."

The village hall, not far from Inverewe, served as an outlying surgery and had ENT forceps and head mirror. I left my hosts (telling them to keep the Venison hot) and drove towards the village remembering an event from my early schooldays when a pupil panicked after lodging a pencil rubber in his nose.

As I approached the surgery, I encountered a sight I shall never forget. Driving towards me in an open topped Morris Minor was a distraught young woman and sitting in the passenger seat, her husband, clutching the handle of a 4-pronged GRAIP (or garden fork), one prong through his cheek, one through his nose!

The Scot's doctor had forgotten his vernacular!

# Man'ure Destined to Make Compost

One wild March day, I was called to the home of a well known retired Neurosurgeon in Badachro where the lady of the house had slipped on the ice and injured her arm. I was greeted at the door by the patient whose arm was in a silk scarf sling and who bade me enter, handed me a cheese grater saying "I want to finish making Wylie's lunch before you send me off to Inverness for the x-ray".

Suddenly a wet souwesterly blew open the back door bringing with it Sir Wylie MacKissock in dripping jumper and kilt, clutching a soil laden armful of vegetables. Because of his macular degeneration he did not see me and immediately turned to wash the produce calling over his shoulder "Go and lie down till the doctor comes, I'm making lunch".

Then, still in his waterproof and dripping hat stirring the white sauce, I came into his field of vision. "Ah you're the young man who likes trees. Come with me." Out he went into the gale and he led me to a magnificent 40 foot Eucalyptus. "Put your arms round the trunk lad. Plant Eucalyptus if you want to do that in your lifetime." He then led me to the biggest compost heap I have seen and pushed my hand into its centre and told me to take out a handful.

This he thrust in front of my nose saying "How does that smell?" "Odourless and beautifully textured" I replied. "And two of my old dead dogs went into its making. Only their jaw bones remained after a few years. Make compost my lad!"

# Community Care

Sleet was blowing off the white tops of the Atlantic breakers on to the steep single track road winding down from Gruinard Bay. It was nearly midnight on a Friday in December when the policeman awoke me. "There's been an accident above Gruinard, we'll drive over together."

The scene was awesome. Through the driving sleet torchlights illuminated a heavy truck suspended precariously on top of an overturned Land Rover which had been reduced to 50% of its height, all facing down a steep icy road. Cries of distress were audible from within. Royal Marines in both vehicles had been travelling to undergo winter training and one had "overtaken" the other. The nearest lifting gear and ambulance was almost an hour away. Fortunately it was now early Saturday rather than the Sabbath and half a mile down the road, Donald MacLean, an engineer home on leave from Dubai and acting as barman in his own hotel was still serving customers. All hands and somewhat unsteady feet were enlisted and it was remarkable to see a dry stone dyke transformed into a jack enabling us to extract the living and the dead.

By 6 am after we had completed the rescue and care, the ambulance and fire engine departed. "You'll be coming back with me for a dram after all that" Donald announced to the rescue team. I remember trying to focus on the clock behind the bar at about 9 am and saying that patients will be waiting for me at the surgery. "Och I wouldn't be worrying doctor" was Donald's reply. Somehow I drove to the surgery, was met by the housekeeper and I apologised and told her to send the first patient into my room "Oh don't you worry doctor, you'll have a cup of tea first".

The next thing I remember is gazing up at the ceiling and wonder how I came to be lying in damp clothes on the examination couch at 3pm. I found the housekeeper and asked about the patients. "Oh, there were no patients doctor. They heard you'd been busy." I received no calls for the remainder of the weekend!

# Tim Melville-Ross

*Tim Melville-Ross was Chief Executive of the Nationwide Building Society 1985-1994, having joined the Society first in 1974. He was appointed Director-General of the Institute of Directors in 1994 and in 1999 became Chairman of Investors in People, UK. He is a Director of several companies including DTZ plc, Bovis Homes plc, Royal London Insurance and Newscast Limited. He is Council member of the Institute of Business Ethics and the University of Essex and is a Trustee of Uppingham School.*

# An Open Secret

s Chief Executive of Nationwide Building Society, I had expected to be challenged by many new tasks, but not one where I would have to entertain an audience of two thousand with no props or rehearsal at all.

Discretion was obviously going to be a requirement in the top job, especially in the very early stages of key corporate negotiations. So it was key in the approach I made to my opposite number at the Anglia Building Society, Tony Stoughton-Harris, suggesting we should merge our two organisations. There was to be nobody else involved until we had worked out an outline plan - at least that was the idea, but I am anticipating the entertainment.

When the merger was almost complete, Tony and I arranged a conference at the Wembley Conference Centre for the 2,000 most senior people in the organisation to tell them all about it. The centre-piece of the event was meant to be a double act by Tony and myself immediately after lunch, when we would respond to questions which had been filmed in "vox pop" fashion during the lunch interval. All was set, only for us to find that the technology didn't work, so we had a large audience to entertain, and nothing to do it with.

Something Tony said as we struggled to think how to cope with this rather unpromising situation reminded me of one of his earliest experiences as we began our "secret" merger discussions, so I told the audience about it, which kept us going until someone fixed the technology. Anxious to find out more about Nationwide, but unable to ask too many questions for fear of starting rumours, Tony decided to visit a Nationwide branch incognito. Hat pulled down over his eyes, coat collar up, he sidled up to the counter and asked a staff member for information about the Society. "Oh hello, Mr Stoughton-Harris," she said, "what are you doing in here?"

The best laid plans of mice and men.

# Graham Millard

*Graham Millard started in the NHS 43 years ago entering via The National Training Scheme. Senior appointments have included being the first Administrator of the Royal Cornwall Hospital (Treliske), Administrator of Northwick Park Hospital (1974-84) and District General Manager in West Dorset (1985-87). He was Tutor to the National Training Scheme at Manchester University (1967-69) and currently is a Non-Executive Director of North Dorset Primary Care NHS Trust and a management consultant.*

*In addition to general management, he maintains a continuing interest in personnel management which gave rise to two publications on the subject. He is author of the King's Fund book on 'Commissioning' having commissioned two new hospitals at Treliske and Northwick Park.*

*He is a School Governor and a Church Warden, plays keyboard and composes music. He and his wife Margaret, live in the delightful Dorset village of Sydling St. Nicholas and he remains an enthusiast for the NHS, having gained, as he says, "many lasting friendships, considerable fun and fulfilment".*

# Covered in Soap

M y first major mistake in the NHS occurred at the Royal Hospital Richmond where my duties included ordering the hospital's supplies. Having noticed we were running low on yellow soap - down to only 10 bars - I immediately reordered three gross. A week later the goods were delivered. A few minutes after arrival, I was summoned to the store. "Who ordered this lot?", I was asked. The entire basement area was overflowing with soap. What I hadn't realised is that yellow soap was supplied in five foot lengths - 432 of them! The soap lasted longer than I did at Richmond Hospital!

# The Line, the Hitch and the Wardrobe

A nother incident I remember well occurred three years later, working as Administrator of the Memorial Hospital, Woolwich. The scene is my office, originally a doctor's bedroom. This is significant because it contained a built-in wardrobe.

Over lunch I heard that Mr Wallis, a very irritating medical sales representative, was visiting the hospital. I alerted my trusty deputy to protect me from being visited and settled down for my afternoon's work.

To my horror at 3 o'clock I heard Mr Wallis's voice in the corridor and my deputy insisting I was out all day. Unfortunately my door was half open, allowing Mr Wallis to see a teacup on my desk. "Mr Millard must be here", he insisted "there's his tea". Mr Wallis, closely chaperoned by my deputy, was about to enter.

There was only one solution, that was to get inside the wardrobe packed tight with stationery. Bent double, gripping the door by its frame I thought I was safe. Suddenly the situation deteriorated: Mr Wallis entered my office and sat down. Terrified that I might sneeze and numb with tension I remained in the wardrobe for ten minutes.

The end was worthy of Whitehall farce when I decided I must emerge. I had persuaded myself that Mr Wallis might just believe that the wardrobe was an entrance to an underground tunnel - perhaps even a nuclear bunker! I leapt from my foetal position, crashed out of the cupboard with one foot in a brown box. Having had several minutes to rehearse some suitable lines, I blurted out "I hope I haven't kept you waiting. I've been down the tunnel stock taking."

I felt obliged to place a larger order than usual for his products and Mr Wallis left in a state of shock. Ever since I have insisted only to see representatives by appointment!

# Sir John Mortimer

*John Mortimer, an only child, grew up in Buckinghamshire. He attended Harrow School then read law at Oxford University. A playwright, novelist and QC, he spent many years as a practising barrister but gave up law in the 1980's after the success of the Rumpole books based on his TV series, Rumpole of the Bailey. His other books include "Titmuss Regained" and "Felix in the Underworld". His first book, Charade, a black comedy was published in 1947.*

# Rumpole and the Actor Laddie

M r Rumpole. Your Timing! My dear, it's something to die for. And the hand gestures! So telling. That wonderful sniff of contempt, just the way Larry used to do in 'The Merchant'. Of course, I've only had the opportunity of seeing your perf from the gods, the public gallery that is, at the Old Bailey. And I don't believe you saw the last thing I did. My Adam the gardener in 'As You' with the Clithero Mummers. A small part, of course, but I think I made a little jewel of it. That was in 84, or was it 85? It's difficult to get cast when you're not young, and definitely not prepared to take your clothes off. That's why I'm thrilled that we're working together at last. I've dreamed and dreamed, I promise you, my dear, of playing opposite the great Rumpole of the Bailey!

Was my timing so good? Quite honestly I had never thought about it. And yet I was half pleased to get a tribute from the client who had told me at the outset that he was 'in the business', and when I asked what business that might be, he had given a light laugh and said, 'A poor player, an honour I share with Garrick and Irving and the late, great Sir Donald Wolfit. My crown is a little tarnished now, but some old-theatre-goers won't easily forget my Benvolio, my French Ambassador, above all my Rosencrantz in the Danish play. I have, it's true, been resting for, well to be honest with you, getting on for quite a while, which is why I'm so looking forward to our forthcoming engagement. I know I haven't lost the trick of holding an audience. I just hope I won't have trouble remembering "the lines". I fear I'm no longer the "quick study" I was.

The elderly man, talking with the volubility of someone emerging from years of silence, had a pink face, a monkish fringe of grey hair and the appearance of an elderly cherub run to fat. He wore a light grey suit, stained at the buttons, suede shoes and a bright pink tie. A voluminous silk handkerchief billowed from his breast pocket and he smelt of some pungently seductive eau de toilette. His name, inscribed on my brief, was Percival Delabere and the venue in which we were to perform together was, I am sorry to say, the London Sessions, where Percival was engaged to play the lead on a fairly ordinary charge of theft.

When he was no longer, as he would say, "in demand" as an actor, Percy Delabere, ("Call me Percy, dear boy") Johnny G and Dame Edith always did, eked out his living on a small income left to him by an aunt and occasional speech lessons to puzzled West Indians or Spanish waiters who wanted to talk the singsong tones of the long-dead actor-managers. He was able to afford a bedsitting room on the top floor of a crumbling Victorian house in Talbot Square, near to Paddington Station. This undesirable residence was the property of a Miss Hunter, a large, untidy woman, a solitary gin drinker whose quarters and financial affairs were in a perpetual muddle. She fussed over her younger, more attractive tenants and took only a perfunctory interest in the fading career of the old actor on the top floor.

The circumstances which led to our meeting, and his complimentary remarks about my perf, in the conference room at the London Sessions, were unfortunate. During his long rests it was Percy's practice to wander about the house, going into other people's rooms in order to bore them with reminiscences of Larry, John G and the great Sir Donald Wolfit. On the afternoon in question, Miss Hunter had wandered round to the off-licence and left the door open. It was agreed that Percy had popped into her room to pay his rent and, apparently for want of anything better to do, had examined some items of the landlady's jewellery which she had left in a jumble of possessions on a marble-topped table under a tarnished mirror. A Mr Crookshank, a retired insurance salesman, had passed Miss Hunter's open door and seen Percy slip her most valued possession, a diamond and emerald ring, on to one podgy finger and stand admiring the effect of it in the looking glass. Later Miss Hunter announced the ring missing and Percy made a considerable investment in new pink shirts, a silk dressing gown and a purple spotted bow tie from a posh shop in Jermyn Street.

'How did you afford all that?' I asked Percival.

'Poor as I am, Mr Rumpole, I had made savings. And one must keep up appearances. That is very important. You never get offered anything if you don't keep up appearances.'

I thought that producers would hardly be hurrying to Percival's door on the hot news that he had bought a new dressing gown, but I didn't say so. Instead I came to the very heart, the nub of the matter. 'I suppose you'd better tell me now. Did you take the landlady's ring?'

'Mr Rumpole.' There followed a long pause, which, although no doubt meant to be dramatic, soon became tedious. And then, 'Do you really have such a low view of my profession?'

Ignoring the fact that he seemed to find no appreciable difference between the bar and the stage, I did my best to focus the man's attention. 'That's a question you'll have to answer "Yes" or "No" soon.'

'Not now, Mr Rumpole.' He held up a warning hand. 'I shall tell the full story when I enter the witness box.'

'You'd better not enter it until I know what you're going to say.'

'My dear! Would you deny me the witness box? Am I to be a mere extra, a super, a spear carrier with no lines? My crown may be a little tarnished now but I think you can rely on me to play the lead. A promise I shall not disappoint.'

'You'll go into the witness box over my dead body, ' was what I should have said; but I weakly agreed to call him. How could I deny the old actor landing the only leading role he was likely to get?

I did say, 'I assume you'd deny keeping the ring?'

'Mr Rumpole. It's for you to make assumptions. It's for me to play the lead. To the best of my poor ability.' And that is, of course, exactly what he did.

'Mr Rumpole. Can't you control your client?'

'I'm afraid, your Honour, that is quite impossible.'

Why had I ever allowed Percival to take centre stage? We were a quarter of an hour into his evidence, he was in full flow and his Honour Judge Archibald, 'artful Archie' to his many detractors, owing to his many ingenious ways of persuading juries to convict, was clearly in the throes of terminal irritation.

The trial had started quietly.

Miss Hunter, voluminous and somewhat confused, told the story of the missing ring which Mr Crookshank had last seen on Percy's finger. And then Percy had gone into the witness box and taken the oath in the hushed tones of the Prince of Denmark addressing his father's ghost. After a few routine questions he ignored me and became Mark Antony, orating to the Roman plebs.

'My friends and fellow countrymen on the jury, ' his voice was low and throbbing. 'May I take a moment of your time to speak of my all too humble self. I am a poor player that struts and frets his hour upon the stage, in my case this witness box, and then perhaps to your relief, will be heard no more. I have lived, it is no exaggeration to say, for my art. I have done my poor best to dedicate myself to that perpetual challenge which is the theatre. I have sung with Shakespeare and argued with Shaw and, yes, I am not ashamed to confess it, on occasions lost my trousers with Ray Cooney.' Here he waited for a laugh which never came. 'Such a career teaches passion. It teaches love of the language. What it cannot teach is sensible behaviour and self-restraint...'

After a good deal more in the same vein, Artful Archie, having made his irritated interjection, attempted to drag the wandering thespian back to the point in issue. So I put the question to him bluntly.

'Mr Delabere. Do you agree that you put Miss Hunter's ring on your finger and surveyed the effect in the mirror?'

'Members of the jury. You will remember the line in the Moorish play - I mean Othello - about the base Indian who threw a pearl away, richer than all his tribe?'

'Mr Delabere!' I have to confess that the Rumpole patience, never my strongest asset, was wearing extremely thin. 'Let's forget the Moorish play, the Danish play, or indeed the Scottish play for a moment and concentrate on one simple fact. Did you put Miss Hunter's ring upon your finger?'

'I imagined, for a moment, that I was playing Doge in the Venetian play. I remembered that they were rich in jewellery.'

'For the last time, Did you put on the ring or not?'

'I did.'

The relief at actually getting an answer gave me the confidence to move on to the next, most dangerous question, 'And did you take it away with you, Mr Delabere? Did you steal it?'

Percy treated us to one of his famous pauses, during which I held my breath and Archie sat with his pencil poised to take a note. When Percy spoke again it was to treat us to yet another oration.

'Members of the jury. I have taken the liberty of calling myself a poor player and poor I am. It has been a constant worry to keep myself in those few necessities, a good suit, a few decent shirts, an attractive tie, which are necessary to be in the swim, to be seen and thought of as a character actor, now my juvenile days are over, who is constantly "available." Those who devote themselves to their art do not expect to be richly rewarded. We don't ask for yachts, members of the jury, or old master paintings, or a Rolls-Royce motorcar. What we, perhaps, have the right to expect is a decent standard of living, which would leave us free to dream, to create, to study and, when in work, do our job without the haunting fear of future poverty. So what am I saying? Did I steal the ring? Yes. I stole the ring. I announce it publicly! I announce it proudly. Miss Hunter has boxes of jewellery, most of which she never wears. You have seen her, her fingers are glittering, her neck is loaded, with semiprecious trinkets. That ring, members of the jury, is the tribute the property owner pays to the artist. Judge me if you will. Call me guilty if you must. But don't deny me your understanding or your mercy, which, like the fairness of the Almighty, transcends all human laws!'

At which point, I promise you, Percy Delabere clung to the front of the witness box and bowed as though acknowledging the wildest applause after the most exhausting performance. The jury sat in stolid silence and the only voice heard was that of Artful Archie, who sounded content that my client had convicted himself without needing any assistance from the learned judge. 'Mr Rumpole, I imagine you will now advise your client to change his plea.'

'I see it's nearly one o'clock.' I decided to play for time, 'Perhaps I might take instructions during the lunch-time adjournment?'

'Very well. But in view of what he has told us, I must cancel his bail. Delabere will be taken down to the cells. Back here at two o'clock, members of the jury.'

Confronting the actor Laddie in the cells before having a drink would have been like having an operation without an anaesthetic and I decided against it. I ordered a pint of Guinness in the pub across the road and was about to consume it with a slice of pork pie and pickle, when 'Spider' Wilkinson, the counsel for the Prosecution, so called because of his thin arms and legs which seemed to stretch out in all directions and in his solemn, bespectacled face, came in and greeted me with, 'Rumpole! You lucky bastard!'

'Lucky? To have a client who is so clean off his head that he makes a totally unnecessary confession to the jury in a performance of such unutterable harm that I blushed to hear it? Do you know that idiotic old actor complimented me on my timing! His timing was perfectly judged to get him a long rest in Wormwood Scrubs.'

'Did you think you could get him off?'

'We had a chance. There was no evidence he actually sold the ring, or even kept it.'

'He didn't.'

'What do you mean?'

'Just that! Dear old Miss Hunter searched through her handbag, apparently a lengthy undertaking, late this morning and found a receipt from a jeweller. She'd taken the ring in to be repaired long after your client tried it on. We rang the shop and it's still there. When we go back I'll have to tell Archie. He's not going to like it.'

Strangely enough, when I brought the good news to Percy, he also seemed disappointed. When I asked him why on earth he'd shopped himself to the jury, I could make no sense of his reply. 'It seemed right somehow, Mr Rumpole. The perfect dramatic ending to what I flatter myself was a moving speech, powerfully performed. I stood before them, I thought, a heroic victim and not a foolish old actor who tried rings on for fun. I think it was my finest performance.'

I left Percy Delabere then, having resolved never under any circumstances, to work with him again.

*Reproduced by kind permission*
*of the author and Advanpress Limited*

# Terry Neill

*Terry Neill was born in Belfast, Northern Ireland. He was Captain of Northern Ireland, Arsenal and Hull City Football clubs and became Manager of Northern Ireland, Arsenal, Tottenham Hotspur and Hull City. He was the youngest Manager of all these clubs. He transferred from Bangor (N.I.) to Arsenal in 1959. He scored the winning goal for Northern Ireland against England on his 50th cap and as Player/Manager.*

# True Stories from the Pitch

George Best and Miss World return to their hotel after a night out in a casino.

George has won a significant amount and ordered some champagne, whilst Miss World goes to the bathroom. The hotel porter arrives with the champagne - George had thrown wads of money onto the bed - Miss World emerges from the bathroom wearing a short see through night-dress. The porter politely asks George the question - "George, where did it all go wrong?!"

*Irish selector discussing young international prospect:*
   "He has talent and might be O.K. when he manures!"

*Danny Blanchflower circa. 1960:*
   "Why don't we play across the pitch and get the match over early?"

*A man walking through a graveyard notices a tombstone inscription:*
   "Here lies a football director and an honest man" - thinks - that's a novel idea burying two people in the same grave!

*Chairman to Manager:* "Don't worry I'm right behind you."
*Manager to Chairman:* "I'd rather you were in front of me where I can see you!"

# The Rt. Hon. The Lord Owen

*Lord Owen's current activities include Chairman of New Europe, Chancellor of the University of Liverpool, Director of the Centre for International Health and Co-operation and member of the Eminent Persons Group on Curbing Illicit Trafficking in Small Arms and Light Weapons.*

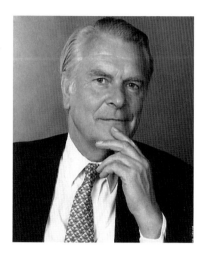

*Lord Owen's business interests include being Executive Chairman of Middlesex Holdings, a metal trading company with interests in Russia and other CIS countries, a Director of EuropeSteel.com; a non-executive Director of Coats Viyella; non-executive Director of the US pharmaceutical company Abbott Laboratories and a non-executive Director of New Crane Publishing.*

*From 1992-95 Lord Owen was the EU Co-Chairman of the International Conference on former Yugoslavia.*

*He was created a Life Baron - Lord Owen of the City of Plymouth - in the Dissolution Honours of 1992 and he was made a Companion of Honour in the Queen's Birthday Honours in June 1994.*

*David Owen was a Member of Parliament for 26 years during which, under Labour Governments, he was Navy Minister, Health Minister and Foreign Secretary. He was a founder of the Social Democratic Party in 1981 and its leader from 1983-90.*

*Educated at Sidney Sussex College, Cambridge and St Thomas's Hospital, London, David Owen was a neurologist and Research Fellow on the Medical Unit before entering Parliament in 1966.*

*Lord Owen has written a number of books including 'Human Rights' (1978), 'Face the Future' (1981), his autobiography 'Time to Declare' (1991), an anthology of poetry 'Seven Ages' (1992) and 'Balkan Odyssey' (1995).*

# An Extraordinary Coincidence

My parliamentary career started in 1962 more or less in the same week as my becoming a newly qualified doctor. The South-West Regional Labour Party wrote to ask if I had any objection to my being shortlisted for the Torrington parliamentary seat. I rang up the Office and asked what was involved and on being told that it did not mean much more, if selected, than going down to Torrington one weekend a month, I agreed that my name could go forward. Even so, my decision to accept nomination was a pretty extraordinary one since most junior doctors find little time for anything else during this hectic period in their lives. I decided not to tell anyone in the hospital of my candidacy. I was intent on a serious medical career and felt that if the consultants knew that I was involved in politics they would not consider I was really committed to medicine. Much to my surprise I was chosen to fight the seat. The sitting MP was Percy Browne who had won it back for the Conservatives in the 1959 General Election from the Liberal. He was a popular local farmer and steeplechase jockey who had taken part in the Grand National.

One night when I was on duty in St Thomas's Hospital, an extraordinary coincidence took place. I was asked by a friend to look after one of his patients who had been admitted that day, very seriously ill. He mentioned the patient was a Conservative MP and had a nasty thrombosis in his lungs. When I went to see the patient he was asleep with his face turned away from me. I picked up his wrist to take his pulse and literally gasped when I read his name tag. The man lying in front of me was Percy Brown, the MP for Torrington. I urgently telephoned a friend and got him out of bed moaning and groaning to take over responsibility. Having this particular MP dead on my hands would have been very embarrassing. Fortunately Percy Browne survived and I used to drop in and chat to him as he recovered. Like most people I became captivated by his charm and I was very glad when he stood down on health grounds which ensured I never had to campaign against him.

# Squadron Leader John Peters     Gulf War POW 1991

*John Peters was born in London. He joined the RAF in 1980 as a university cadet and graduated from Manchester University in 1983. In 1987, he became a staff pilot at the Air Navigation School, RAF Finningley. In 1988 he converted to Tornado GR1s and was posted to XV Squadron Laarbruch in Germany; the Squadron was subsequently involved in the Gulf War. He has written two best-selling books on his experiences and is an international conference speaker.*

*After another tour at RAF Bruggen on 31 Squadron, he returned to England in 1993 to become an instructor pilot at the Tri-national Tornado Training Establishment, RAF Cottesmore, Leicestershire. In 1997 he completed a Masters Degree in Business Administration at Leicester University. On promotion to squadron leader, he was a mission director on AWACS patrolling the Northern No-Fly zone in Iraq and then became a Flight Safety officer in MOD. On leaving the RAF in 2000, he started a corporate development company. He is married to Helen and has two young children, Guy and Toni.*

# Health Freak!

This was the place where we were going to die. A black, cold, dark interrogation centre in the heart of Saddam's Iraq. We had been beaten for two days. We were still handcuffed, blindfolded, the rifle butts resting on our backs, with the occasional tap on the skull to keep our heads low. The Iraqis brought tea along for us, hot and sweet, in a glass jam jar. This was amazing. You suddenly realised with a rush of saliva that you had not eaten or drunk anything for about forty-eight hours. They offered some to Jeff Zaun.

"Do you want tea?"

"No, Sir," he replied emphatically.

Non-plussed, the Iraqi officer stepped back. How could this prisoner who had had no food or drink for two days refuse hot, sweet tea?

"Why do you not want tea? It is OK, there is nothing wrong with it. Look, I will drink some."

"No, Sir. I cannot drink tea. It's bad for you, It has caffeine in it."(!)

The Iraqis must have realised then that there was no way they were ever going to win! This situation even made me raise a smile, under my black bag. I just couldn't believe, given the circumstances, that he refused the liquid because of its caffeine content. Hell, I do not smoke, never have, but if offered a cigarette, I probably would have had one. Cancer was not my immediate concern at that time.

# François Pienaar

*The eldest of four sons of Jan-Harm Pienaar and Valerie Diana du Toit was born in the district of Drie Riviere (Three Rivers) outside Vereeniging, in South Africa. Read Law at the Rand Afrikaans University (RAU) in Johannesburg and played rugby. Member of the RAU National Club Champions team in 1990 and next played for Transvaal (100 caps, 87 as captain). Represented South Africa in 29 Tests, all as Captain - Won 19, drew 2, lost 8 . Captain of the victorious World Cup team in 1995.*

*Sensationally dropped from the South African side and forced into exile he joined the Watford, Hertfordshire based Saracens first as player-coach and now is Chief Executive. Helped guide the side from a struggling second division team to one of the leading clubs in the English Premiership. Saracens won the 1998 Tetley's Cup against Wasps.*

# The Rugby World Cup

June 24 1995 - the World Cup Final at Ellis Park Stadium in South Africa. Before the start of the game I visited the team doctor Dr Frans Verster and had my ankles strapped. Next a little physiotherapy to stay loose and relaxed and then to the changing room. There I found to my amazement and joy and standing next to my place was none other than President Nelson Mandela wearing a Number 6 Springbok jersey! He beamed at me and shook my hand. I was completely overwhelmed by his presence and the fact that he had taken the time to make such a thoughtful gesture. He walked round the room wishing each and every player good luck and within ten minutes he was gone. I refocussed and then heard what sounded like an explosion in the stadium only to learn that it was a South African Airways jumbo jet that had executed an audacious flypast, passing less than 200 metres above the stadium. After two such spectacular and unexpected events the mood of the players soared and we had to keep reminding ourselves that we had a difficult match ahead of us which would demand our total concentration.

Just before ten to three I led the Springbok team onto the field and a stadium of 63,000 spectators erupted. The emotional charge was so great that I could not sing the national anthem, "Nkosi sikelel i Africa" when it was played, as I knew I would burst into tears and inadvertently encourage the New Zealand players. We survived their haka intact. My other recollections are that the whistle blows, the 80 minutes begin and end 15-12 with a Springbok victory. Now in another surge of emotion I sink to my knees and quietly thank God for this wonderful moment in my life. The bear hugs and tears remain a blur but I remember giving Hennie le Roux one of my closest friends the biggest hug of all.

The atmosphere in the stadium and throughout the country went far beyond sport. It reflected the new spirit of the nation - reconciliation and reunification of a people previously torn apart. I was proud to have played a small part in this joyous day. For me the occasion was inexorably imprinted in my memory when President Mandela handed me the Webb Ellis Trophy, the World Cup, and thanked me "for what the team had done for the country". Fortunately I had the presence of mind to reply "No Sir, it is you that we thank for what you have done".

# The Lord Rix

*Lord Rix was born in Yorkshire. At the age of 18 he became a professional actor and after serving in the RAF during the war, formed his own Theatre Company in 1947. In 1950, he presented "Reluctant Heroes" at the Whitehall Theatre in London and this began a thirty-year run as an actor/manager. He presented and acted in over 70 productions from the Whitehall and Garrick theatres for television and produced and appeared in many film farces.*

*From 1980 to 1987 he was Secretary General of Mencap, becoming its Chairman in 1988. In 1998 he was appointed President, an office he currently holds.*

*His work for people with learning disabilities has been recognised a number of times, receiving a knighthood in 1986 and becoming a life Baron in 1992. He is a very active member of the House of Lords, especially with regard to issues concerning people with learning disabilities.*

*He is married and has 2 sons and 2 daughters. His eldest child has Down's Syndrome and thus his interest in learning disability issues is of an intense personal nature.*

# What's in a Post-Nominal?

Who can resist a courteous letter, espousing a good cause and, above all, correctly addressed - with every post-nominal in place? Not I, for one - and Dr. Goolamali's letter fulfilled all those criteria, hence this ready response.

For those who are uncertain as to what is a post-nominal I can explain quite simply by quoting Dr. Goolamali's own 'M.D. (Lond.), F.R.C.P.' - whilst mine include 'Kt, CBE, DL'. Regrettably, these post-nominals, together with my full title, cause some considerable consternation in the computerised community. By such illustrious companies as Harrods, British Gas, British Telecom and others of a lesser breed with junk-mail catalogues, I have been addressed as 'Dear Lord Rixktcbedl', 'The Rt. Hon. The Lord DL', 'The Lord Tricks' and - must fulsome of all - 'The Lord'.

Pride of place, though, must go to the keyboard operator who probably recalled me from my farcical days. The salutation was simply 'Dear Lord Prick'. My ears did redden at that one, I can tell you...

# Chief Rabbi Professor Jonathan Sacks

*Rabbi Professor Jonathan Sacks has been Chief Rabbi of the United Hebrew Congregations of the Commonwealth since 1 September 1991, the sixth incumbent since 1945.*

*At the time his appointment was announced, he was Principal of Jews' College, London, the world's oldest rabbinical seminary, where he also held the Chair in Modern Jewish Thought and instituted novel programmes in rabbinic ordination from Jews' College as well as from London's Yeshiva Etz Chaim. He has been rabbi of the Golders Green and Marble Arch Synagogues in London.*

*His secular academic career has also been a distinguished one. Educated at Gonville and Caius College, Cambridge, where he obtained first class honours in Philosophy, he pursued postgraduate studies at New College, Oxford and King's College, London. In 1990 he delivered the BBC Reith Lectures on 'The Persistance of Faith'.*

*A notably gifted communicator, the Chief Rabbi is a frequent contributor to radio, television and the national press. He is the author of twelve books, the most recent being 'Celebrating Life' (2000) and 'Radical Then Radical Now' (2000).*

*London born, he has been married to Elaine for 30 years. They have three children, Joshua, Dina and Gila.*

# Once in a While God Lets us See the Script

It was one of those moments when you feel part of something so much larger than yourself. It was the summer of 1999. I'd been invited to open an international sports competition. The participants were part of a global network of Jewish youth clubs called Maccabi. For the first time their European gathering was taking place in Scotland. There were well over a thousand young people from twenty-seven different countries. We began, not with the games themselves, but by celebrating the Sabbath together. It was thrilling to pray in the company of so many - especially after all that had happened to European Jewry in the twentieth century. For the first time we were joined by participants from East Europe, where Jewish life was being rekindled after seventy years of suppression under communist rule. This was the Jewish phoenix, communities long dormant coming to life again.

We were in the old town of Stirling with its ancient castle, where "Braveheart" William Wallace and Robert the Bruce fought their famous battles against the English. Elaine, my wife, and I were staying along with the participants at the University, one of the loveliest campuses in Britain. I'd been there once before, under different circumstances. As the Sabbath began, I told the story.

"Almost exactly thirty years ago, I had just finished university and was applying for my first job. There was a vacancy in the Philosophy Department of Stirling University, and I applied. It was my first job application. I was invited for interview and I came to this building. I didn't get the job. I was disappointed. But I went elsewhere and did other things."

"What would have happened if I'd been successful? I wouldn't have become a rabbi. I wouldn't have become Chief Rabbi. And I wouldn't be here now, because the university is on holiday. I would have missed the largest gathering of Jews ever to have come together in Scotland. What made it possible for me to be here in Stirling today? The fact that thirty years ago I came to Stirling and was turned down for a job. Until now, that rejection hurt. Now I understand that I was part of a different story. So it is so often: bad things turn out to have been necessary steps in an important journey. God is a writer; we are His characters. Once in a while He lets us see the script."

*Reproduced by kind permission from 'Celebrating Life'*
*published by Fount an imprint of HarperCollins Publishing.*

# Brian Saperia

*Before going up to Oxford to read Greats, Brian Saperia spent a year as a prep school teacher - main protégés: a well-known playwright and the captain of the ship that sank the Belgrano. He has spent his whole career in the NHS, of which he is a devout supporter. His first appointment after completing the National Training Scheme for Administrators was as Work Study Officer at the Westminster Hospital where he helped to implement an out patient appointment system - plus ça change! This was followed by a long period at Hillingdon Hospital, culminating in what he regards as perhaps the best years of his career as the Administrator of that District General Hospital and associated facilities, working in close harmony (for the most part) with the Medical Administrator and Matron (those were the days!).*

*On the 1982 administrative reorganisation, he was appointed to the combined post of Planning Officer and Administrator for Psychiatry and Learning Difficulty at Northwick Park Hospital, subsequently taking on a number of supporting roles at Health Authority and, latterly, Trust Board levels. Now semi-retired, he works part time (supposedly) running the Harrow Research Ethics Committee and providing administrative support for the senior medical staff at Northwick Park.*

*He is married to the actress, Diana Brookes, and has two grown up children.*

# The Administrator's Tale

Whether it was the effect of too many retsinas the night before or just drowsiness, I don't know, but when I awoke and tried to stand up on the inflatable mattress which passed for my bed, I toppled off it. I was on one of my folk song collecting expeditions to Greece as a student, staying in a friend's flat halfway up Mount Lycabettos, in the middle of Athens. Now, I can't do without my glasses which were just by my bedside and, blast it, it was on those that I landed, smashing the lenses. We had to move "up country" that day and I needed a replacement pair immediately, if not sooner. My travelling companion suggested that the best place to get advice was the British Embassy (little did we know then that 40 years on he was to become British Ambassador to Greece!). So off I stumbled, bleary eyed and half blind, down the hill to the Embassy. I rushed up to the reception desk and blurted out "Please help me. I need an optician - very urgently." The girl at the counter gave me a cheerful "No problem" and, opening a filing cabinet, took out an index card and wrote down the name and address of someone who she assured me would be able to do something for me. "You tell him Maria from the British Embassy is sending you. Tell him grigora - quick". She gave me a bit of a funny look as I left, but I thought nothing of it and went on my myopic way, back up the hill. Eventually, more by luck than judgement, I found myself at the right address, No. 5 Marathan Street. I squinted at the brass plate outside. That's the name I was looking for - Dr Theodoros Pappadopoulos. But what was this underneath? OBSTETRICIAN.

Now I knew the reason for that funny look - what on earth could that callow and innocent looking English youth be wanting an obstetrician for - and why so urgently...? And how was I going to get a new pair of glasses that same day? Easy, I just somehow found my way to an optician's (no mistake this time) and within the hour they were made up for me!

Then there was the time, again in Athens, when I was lured to a clip joint by a chap who befriended me in the street - but that's another story.

# Dinah Sheridan

*Dinah Nadyejda Mec was born in Hampstead, London, to a German Mother and Russian Father. Her parents were both in St Petersburg at the beginning of the Revolution and met escaping on a boat from Arch angel, to exile in England. After serving in World War 1 they settled and became talented photographers starting with a camera picked up from the mud of a French road. Later they became By Appointment to both the Queen and the Queen Mother. Dinah was their most popular, unpaid model from the age of 13.*

*She was a sickly child, contracting infantile tuberculosis at the age of 5, but was strong enough to follow her desires as an actress by the time she was 12. She danced as a moth and a dragonfly and understudied the leading lady (aged 14!) in "Where The Rainbow Ends" and never looked back. By the time the war broke out she had made seven films, and was the first actress ever to appear on Television, from Alexandra Palace, in October 1936, and appeared in the first live three act play ever televised, in 1938.*

*Dinah has appeared in 27 major films, two of which 'Genevieve' and "The Railway Children" are among the British Film Institute's 'Favourite films of the 20th Century.' Last year she appeared in one of television's 'Jonathan Creek' series as 'an elderly missionary with one leg'. There is no question of retirement!*

# Keeping abreast of the times

In 1951 the film chosen for the Royal Film Performance of that year was "Where No Vultures Fly" in which I was featured and for which I had worked six months in Kenya. It was the era when these special Royal performances were also an opportunity for a stage appearance of American as well as British film artists.

This particular year, there was Fred MacMurray, Dan Duryea, Van Johnson, Jane Russell among many including the British contingent.

The presentation to the Queen, and other members of the Royal family was to take place first, and then the artists were to race round to the dressing rooms at the back of the Odeon Cinema to get into whatever costumes would be worn in the stage production part of the evening. The space provided was very small - just two little rooms, one for the men and one for the ladies. Squashed into this tiny space I could see Phyllis Calvert, Googie Withers, Valerie Hobson (with a Ladiesmaid and a suitcase), and among others Margaret Rutherford bravely finding a small space at the mirror powdering her nose with vigour.

Jane Russell was to sing and had brought a different dress for her spot. The magnificent evening dress in which she had been presented was strapless, unlike the one hanging on a nail into which she was about to change. She unzipped the strapless version, letting it fall round her ankles and suddenly let out a wail: "Jeesus Cherist, I've forgotten my Brazeer!". She stood clad only in her lace panties, in horror, - her magnificent figure very prominent.

There was dead silence in the crowded dressing room, except for the little swishing noises of Margaret Rutherford's powder puff - when the elegant, cool voice of Valerie Hobson broke the shocked silence - "If you wouldn't think it was boasting I could lend you one of mine!"

Sad to say I cannot remember whether the offer was taken up - nor whether it proved adequate!

# Ned Sherrin

*Ned Sherrin changed the face of television in the 60's with 'That Was The Week That Was', which he devised, produced and directed. On film he produced 'The Virgin Soldiers' and many other successful movies. He was nominated for a Tony Award for 'Side by Side by Sondheim' which he directed and in which he starred in the West End and on Broadway. He won an Olivier Award for 'The Ratepayer's Iolanthe'.*

*He has also written many novels and plays including "Beecham", "I Gotta Shoe" and "The Mitford Girls" (with Caryl Brahms). Recent publications include "Theatrical Anecdotes", "Sherrin's Year" and "Scratch and Actor". He presents the highly successful "Loose Ends" on Radio 4. In the Theatre he has directed other notable hits including "Jeffrey Bernard is Unwell" and "Our Song", starring Peter O'Toole, "Mr & Mrs Nobody", with Judi Dench and Michael Williams, "A Passionate Woman" starring Stephanie Cole and "Salad Days".*

*He was made a CBE in the 1997 Queen's New Year's Honours List.*

# Mother's Always Right...

The young Duke of Kent and his sister, are taken to see a famous illusionist in a London music hall. The number ends with some nudity, and the nanny doesn't know what to do. As they leave she ventures to ask, "How did Your Highness enjoy the performance?". "I'm scared." "Why?". "Mama told me if I looked at naked women I'd turn to stone - and it's starting."

*as discovered by Paul Gallagher in Jean Cocteau's diary January 10th, 1953*

# Tears as Souvenirs

Sir Michael Gambon had played Oscar Wilde - on television I think. Soon after he met a "civilian" who said, "Didn't you find it difficult playing a homosexual?".

"No", Gambon replied, leading him on, "You see, I used to be one."

"Why did you stop?"

"Well, it made my eyes water".

# Dr Thomas Stuttaford

*Dr Thomas Stuttaford was born and brought up in rural Norfolk where his father and grandfather had been general practitioners. He joined the family practice in 1959 after completing his national service with the 10th Royal Hussars and medical training at Oxford and London.*

*From 1970-1974 Dr Stuttaford became the Conservative MP for Norwich South while continuing to work as a doctor in London. Since then he has divided his time between occupational health and genito-urinary medicine - for over twenty years he worked at the Royal London Hospital, Moorfields Eye Hospital and the former Queen Mary's Hospital for the East End - and medical journalism.*

*Dr Stuttaford is "The Times" doctor; he has been writing for the paper for seventeen years. He is also a regular contributor to The Oldie magazine, and has in the past been the medical correspondent to Options and Elle magazines. Dr Stuttaford has written two books, To Your Good Health! The Wise Drinker's Guide (1997) and In Your Right Mind, Everyday Psychological Problems and Psychiatric Conditions Explored and Explained (1999) both published by Faber & Faber. He was appointed OBE in 1996.*

# Shotgun Diplomacy

Harry Rowntree was short, wiry, aggressive and a very hard working tractor driver. Social relationships were not his strong suit and his approach to his wife made Andy Capp look like a 'New Man'. His wife - with straight, mousy hair and a figure that drooped in all the wrong places - had four children under seven. She filled what time was left over from looking after them by having miscarriages. I always had a soft spot for Mrs Rowntree and we drank tea together as she described, without complaint, the latest horrors of life with Harry. 'Harry', she explained 'doesn't believe in contraception'. Harry didn't believe either in immunisation programmes, hospitals, modern drugs (he preferred a bottle of 'physic'), antenatal care, health visitors - or me as his local doctor.

One afternoon I received a call from Mrs Rowntree to say that she was bleeding again. By the time I reached her village, five or six miles away, she had already miscarried and it only remained for me to give her an injection, comfort her and clear up the blood-soaked bedroom - under the wide-eyed gaze of the four little Rowntrees, all dressed like urchins in a 1910 Punch cartoon. We'd just made the bedroom spick and span when in came Harry.

He rushed up the stairs, swore at his wife for miscarrying and declared that it was all the fault of the antenatal clinics. Although not a great father, Harry did like the concept of parenthood. He hovered around the top of the stairway which led straight from the downstairs sitting room up to the bedroom. The children started to cry. I promise that I gave him no more than a little push, so that I might take the bucket filled with bloody water downstairs but it must have caught Harry off balance because, with a fearful shout, he fell from top to bottom of the precipitous stairs. There was a low moan, a seemingly long silence and then a slamming of the front door before Harry was gone.

The children continued to cry, but for the first time in years, Mrs Rowntree laughed and laughed and laughed.

Next morning, when I went into the village, I saw Harry on his tractor with a shotgun beside him. He didn't return my jolly wave. The next day he was on a cart, a shotgun across his knees, and someone else was driving the tractor. On the third day he was walking along the street to the pub, shotgun under his arm. He didn't seem to be any more pleased to see me than he was on the day after his wife's miscarriage and my belief in coincidence was beginning to wear thin. Harry, I feared, just could be carrying the gun for my benefit and I went to see his employer. 'Billy', I said 'I don't want to be an alarmist but I just wonder if Harry is carrying his gun with me in mind'. 'Ah, Doctor Tom,' Billy said. 'It is for you but I have made him promise that he will only shoot you in self defence and, that if you don't hit him again, he will spare you'. Harry continued to carry his gun, and his wife continued to have many more children and miscarriages.

That's Jonah in there,
everybody sings in whales!

# Sir Rodney Sweetnam

*Orthopaedic Surgeon to the Queen 1982-92. Sir Rodney, CBE, FRCS is President of the Royal Medical Benevolent Fund. He is a Past President of the Royal College of Surgeons but not a member of the Athenaeum!*

# A Club As Well

Lord Birkenhead, who had never joined, used to annoy the members of the Athenaeum by regularly walking in, going to the lavatory and walking out again. At last, the Committee decided that he should be challenged. On the next occasion, therefore, he was approached by the head porter. "Excuse me Sir, but are you a member of this Club?". Lord Birkenhead looked surprised - "I'm so sorry" he said "but is it a club as well?"

# Sir Donald Tebbit

*Donald Tebbit was born in the small village of Toft, near Cambridge, where his father was a farmer. He was educated at the village elementary school (now closed) and at the Perse School, Cambridge. He was a Scholar at Trinity Hall, Cambridge University. He served in World War II in destroyers (HMSS Quorn, Jason, Vanity and Cockade), returning to the university on demobilization to complete his degree. He entered the Diplomatic Service (then the Foreign Service) by Open Competition in December 1946.*

*From 1946 to 1980 he served alternately at home and overseas in five appointments in the Foreign Office in London and five appointments abroad, which included the Embassy in Washington (twice), the Embassies in Bonn and Copenhagen, and the High Commission in Canberra, Australia.*

*His first appointment in London was in the South American Department when relations with Argentina under General (and Senora!) Peron presented many difficulties at a time when three-quarters of our exiguous meat ration came from that country. His first spell in Washington was under the distinguished Ambassadorship of Sir Oliver Franks when President Truman was in the White House. He next returned to Washington in the role of Minister, the Ambassador's Deputy, when President Nixon was in the White House and Mr Kissinger was dealing with US foreign policy. The last four years of his official life were spent as British High Commissioner in Australia.*

*He was awarded the CMG in 1965, became a KCMG in 1975 and a GCMG in 1980.*

# Priorities

The Episcopalian Minister in Scotland who was surprised and, at the same time, a little gratified, to be asked to visit the sick wife of a staunch Presbyterian Elder. After chatting with her, he was saying goodbye to her husband when curiosity got the better of him. "I was pleased to come", he said, "but why didn't you send for your own Minister?" "Oh, we couldn't risk him", came the reply. "You see, it's typhoid!"

A lady was displeased to find herself placed below her proper place of precedence at an Ambassador's dinner party. When she complained the placement for the whole table had to be re-arranged and she was in due course seated next to the Ambassador. By this time she was feeling slightly conscience-stricken at the trouble she had caused. So she said to the Ambassador: "I am afraid you and your wife must find these questions of precedence highly troublesome". "Oh, not really", replied the Ambassador. "We have always found that people who matter don't mind and people who mind don't matter."

There is this tale of the man who was happily married for 35 years. Then, suddenly, his wife died. About a year later, he met and fell in love with a beautiful girl, many years younger than himself. Eventually he overcame his scruples and proposed to her. She rejected him at first but in the end accepted him but only on condition that he lose 2 stones in weight and get himself fitted up with a hair-piece and contact lenses. He worked at it and eventually met the conditions. The wedding took place and the couple flew to Hawaii for the honeymoon. Exhilarated after a blissful night, he strolled out on to the beach before breakfast. There he was struck by a sudden bolt of lightning and killed outright... Arriving at heaven's gate, he could not refrain from complaining politely to Saint Peter that, after all he had done to achieve happiness, he should have been snatched so quickly and cruelly away. "Why did you do it to me?", he asked indignantly. "I'm terribly sorry", replied St. Peter, "but we just didn't recognise you".

# Dr David Tyrrell

*David Tyrrell, CBE, FRS, was born in Ashford, Middlesex and graduated from Sheffield University. After three years at the Rockefeller Institute and Hospital in New York he joined the staff of the Medical Research Council in 1954 moving to the Common Cold Unit, Salisbury in 1957. He was appointed to the Clinical Research Centre, Harrow from 1967 to 1981, retiring from Salisbury in 1990.*

*He has worked as a physician and laboratory virologist and published papers and books on viruses and other infections of man. He served as member and Chairman of many committees including some on vaccination, AIDS, BSE and laboratory safety and received sundry awards for his work.*

# The Tortuous Course of One's True Love

For many years I worked at the Medical Research Council (MRC) Common Cold Unit on the Downs just outside Salisbury in Wiltshire. Volunteers old and young came there to be inoculated with nose drops containing cold viruses. We then observed and recorded their clinical response. Of course, these experiments were only valid if they were not confused by colds caught naturally from other volunteers or members of the public. So all volunteers lived, usually in pairs, in separate huts, though male and female could only share a flat if they were married.

There were also firm rules for ensuring isolation. They could only talk, or rather shout, to other volunteers through a closed window or at a distance of at least 30 feet, (metrication came later), or they could use the telephone. The penalty for any breach was to immediately leave the trials, and thus their free holiday.

One couple, much in love, wanted to have time together - or as nearly as the rules permitted. They devised a scheme to go on walks together holding opposite ends of a 30ft piece of string, keeping it taut. They started out across the fields and all was well, but then they entered a wood and passed on opposite sides of a tree. They had not reckoned on what would happen!

Local history (or legend) does not record whether they met face to face or whether they stayed at the Unit or were sent home.

# Roger M Uttley

*A former schools and senior international rugby player for England, Roger Uttley, OBE, was first capped in 1973 and went on to win 23 caps, captaining the side 5 times. He played in all 4 tests of the unbeaten British Lions side that toured South Africa in 1974 and was a member of the England grand slam winning side in 1980-81.*

*On retirement from playing, he became a senior RFU coach and was successfully involved with the London Division side before moving on to assistant coach with the 1989 Lions to Australia and coach to England including The World Cup final against Australia.*

*He qualified as a teacher of physical education from Northumberland College of Education in 1971 and taught at Whitley Bay Grammar School and Cramlington High School. Appeared as a competitor in the BBC's Superstars and Superteams and latterly as the programmes referee. Also competed in the first programme of "Survival of the Fittest".*

*Currently director of Physical Education at Harrow School and master in charge of Rugby Football. He is also contracted by the RFU, through Harrow, and managed the England National side to the 1999 Rugby World Cup. Was awarded the OBE for services to rugby in 1991. He is an active patron of several charities most notably SPARKS (Sport Aiding medical Research for Kids) where he has been a council member of several years and served as national President throughout 1997.*

# Traction, Tiddlywinks and Teacher

In 1977 at the age of 27 I suffered a huge blow to my sporting career. The British Lions Rugby team was about to leave home shores for a four match test series of New Zealand. As that season's captain of England I had done enough to gain selection for the tour but had taken some heavy physical knocks in the process.

This manifested itself as the tour party assembled for a training session immediately prior to departure. Whilst I was able to complete the session, soon afterwards I could not sit down or stand up without feeling pain in my lower back. After twenty-four hours and no improvement I had to inform the team management of my predicament. Medical advice was sought. The result was that as the team flew out from Heathrow en-route to Auckland I made the rather shorter flight back to Newcastle. Further investigation confirmed that I had suffered a prolapsed disc. Initial prognosis was that I should begin to re-think my future as a teacher of physical education and could certainly forget about my sporting career as an international rugby player!

The next 18 months were very difficult. For the early period I was bedridden and on traction. Once this form of treatment failed to produce any sign of improvement I then progressed through the whole range of orthodox and alternative forms of treatment in order to try and regain some physical well being.

Improvement came with time. No blinding revelations occurred. It was more a question of two steps forward, one step back, most of the time. Some forms of treatment gave more relief than others; a strategically placed hot water bottle was great for short-term comfort. I learnt the hard way that you can have too much treatment. I also learnt that flexibility played a vital part in maintaining one's level of fitness and also in reducing the risk of injury. Fundamentally, however, time was the great healer coupled with my desire just to move again and exercise in an unrestricted and pain free manner.

This I was finally able to do. I had been advised to begin with that I should take up tiddlywinks but I was eventually able to regain my international place and enjoy the satisfaction of winning a 5 nations Championship and Grand Slam, England's first for 22 years. Now 23 years on I am still teaching physical education and battling to keep the ageing joints moving, trying to strike the difficult balance between keeping fit and not doing too much damage to the body in the process.

Like many sportsmen and women and rugby players in particular I, for one, have every reason to be grateful to the medical profession for the care, attention and good advice over the years - honest!

Some of you potential Nobel Prize winners
are still confusing DNA with C&A!

# Lord Walton of Detchant

*John Walton (Lord Walton of Detchant) qualified at the Newcastle Medical School of the University of Durham in 1945 with first class honours. He was formerly Consultant Neurologist to the Newcastle-upon-Tyne Hospitals, Professor of Neurology in the University, and from 1971-81 Dean of Medicine. From 1983-89, he was Warden of Green College, Oxford. He became a Knight Bachelor in 1979 and was awarded a Life Peerage as Lord Walton of Detchant in 1989. He was President of the British Medical Association from 1980-82, of the Royal Society of Medicine from 1984-86, of the General Medical Council from 1982-89, and of the World Federation of Neurology from 1989-1997. He chaired the House of Lords Select Committee on Medical Ethics and is a member of its Select Committee on Science and Technology. Most recently he has chaired an inquiry on behalf of the latter Committee into Complementary and Alternative Medicine.*

# Professor Henry Miller

Three of the most memorable "Henry Millerisms" emanate from the late Dr. Henry Miller, who was my predecessor as Professor of Neurology and Dean of Medicine in Newcastle and who subsequently became its Vice-Chancellor.

1. The only instrument for eliciting the plantar response (a clinical neurological test when the sole of the foot is stroked with a blunt pointed object) is the ignition key of a Bentley.

2. Whenever a patient consults me with dizziness, I send him to my registrar.

3. Doctors who smoke should be struck off the register.

In his early days, Henry, who dressed in black jacket, grey waistcoat and pin-stripe trousers with carnation in the button-hole and who was remarkably slim, was known generally as "Henry Gorgeous Miller". On one occasion, when I was his registrar, following him with a retinue on a teaching round, we gathered round a bed and the Geordie in the next bed took one look at him and said "Eh, what a toff; I wonder what he wears on Sundays".

Sam Shuster, Professor of Dermatology, when also President of the Students' Medical Society in Newcastle, gave a very racy Presidential Address, during which, at a time when Henry Miller was the vigorous Dean of the Medical School, Sam showed a photograph of the Holbein portrait of Henry VIII with Henry Miller's face in the centre of it and underneath, the caption, "Henry IX".

# U-Turn

Another of my teachers was the late Dr. Alan Ogilvie, a fine chest physician and a delightful man who nevertheless was very absent-minded. On one occasion a patient consulted him in out-patients about a problem with his waterworks, and Dr. Ogilvie said "Can you start all right? Can you stop all right? Can you reverse? - Oh, I'm sorry, I was thinking about my car!"

# Pause for Thought

Then there's the story of the elderly bishop who, at a time when bishops in the Church of England were not required to retire, had a tendency to rise earlier and earlier in the morning. One morning he went downstairs to find the local paper sitting on his doormat at about 6.00am. He was astonished to read on the front page a notice of his own death and inside a long obituary notice, some of which he read with pleasure and some with alarm and annoyance. He felt that he must share this with a member of his flock, so he went to the telephone and spoke to one of his vicars, who answered in a very sleepy voice. The bishop said "Are you up yet?", to which the vicar responded "Oh no, my Lord". "Do you take the local paper?". "Oh yes, my Lord". "Have you seen it?". "No, my Lord." "Well, get hold of it. You'll see on the front page a notice of my death and inside a long obituary notice". There was a long pause. "Where are you ringing from, my Lord?"

# Professor Sir David Weatherall

*Presently Regius Professor of Medicine and Honorary Director of the Institute of Molecular Medicine, University of Oxford. He is also an Honorary Consultant Physician for Oxfordshire District Health Authority and Honorary Director, MRC Molecular Haematology Unit, University of Oxford. Formerly, Nuffield Professor of Clinical Medicine, University of Oxford, 1974-1992 and Professor of Haematology, University of Liverpool, 1971-1974.*

*He was made Knight Bachelor in 1987 and became Commandeur de l'Ordre de la Couronne in 1994. He has received 20 Honorary Degrees.*

*Professor Sir David Weatherall's major research contributions, resulting in over 700 publications, have been in the elucidation of the clinical, biochemical and molecular*

Photograph of a future Regius Professor of Medicine (not Surgery), taken on the roof of the Empire Theatre, Liverpool, in 1954. The facial appearance is not enhanced by the orders of the Director of The Festival Ballet that eunuchs must blow out their cheeks at all times!

*heterogeneity of the thalassaemias and the application of this information to the development of programmes for the prevention of these diseases in different populations throughout the world.*

*Professor Weatherall has, in the last nine or ten years with the MRC, ICRF, Wellcome Trust, E.P. Abraham Research Fund, Nuffield Medical Trustees of the University of Oxford and other charitable bodies, been responsible for the development of the Institute of Molecular Medicine in Oxford. This building houses several groups wishing to apply the new techniques of molecular and cell biology to the study of human disease.*

# A Brief Career as a Eunuch

The only time I had serious doubts about whether to pursue a career in medicine was after, as a student, I had danced with the Festival Ballet in three performances of Sheherazade at the Empire Theatre, Liverpool, in 1954.

One morning, after completing a pharmacology practical class in which we had learnt to roll pills and make haemorrhoid ointment, we walked over to the Students Union to hear a voice on the loudspeaker saying that ten extras were required at the Empire Theatre within the next hour. Leaving a message that we would not be attending the Cardiac Clinic that afternoon because we would be on stage, we rushed down to the theatre and were paraded in a line. A small man with a thick mid-European accent, who, it appears, was the director, informed us that he required seven soldiers and three eunuchs. He wandered along the row and stopped in front of one of my colleagues and said 'you vill be a yenoch'. The expression on my friend's face sent me into convulsions of laughter, whereupon the little man stopped in front of me and said 'you too will be a yenoch'. After a slightly unpleasant scene in which a third 'yenoch' was chosen after threatening legal action against the Company, rehearsals began. During the scene in which the soldiers murder the ladies of the harem one of my more muscular colleagues caused a rather beautiful young ballerina considerable pain by bringing his wooden sword down hard onto the back of her hand. "Don't worry" said the future Professor of Microbiology at a well known London teaching hospital, "this'll fix it". He dug deep into his pocket, produced the ghastly haemorrhoid ointment that he had made earlier that day, and proceeded to rub it onto the back of her hand.

During the matinee performance things did not go entirely to plan for the eunuchs, who had to shuffle on and off the stage with a highly rehearsed 'Yenuch shuffle' on several occasions. At the end of the final act of Sheherazade the leading ballerina stabs herself as the curtain falls. To enable her to do this she is handed a dagger by one of the eunuchs. Each of us were given a rubber dagger to brandish as we shuffled on and off the stage, but one of us was also given a wooden dagger to hand to the ballerina to help her in her final demise. This was to clatter to the ground as the curtain fell and she collapsed. Unfortunately, in the heat of the moment my fellow eunuch handed her his rubber dagger by mistake. Rubber daggers have the habit of bouncing; this one was no exception. It bounced along the stage no less than three times before jumping into the orchestra. But this wasn't the end of the eunuchs' problems. When the curtain falls on the dying ballerina it rises again to show the final scene in frozen stillness. Unfortunately, in our haste to castigate our fellow eunuch for his carelessness we forgot this vital stage direction. We both attacked him and, as the curtain rose to show the final piece of still life, there were three eunuchs having a punch-up; the rest of the cast were frozen as only professional ballet dancers can. The audience fell apart.

Following the two immaculate performances by the eunuchs that followed, and having watched from the wings the goings on between the male and female ballet dancers in the harem scene which is a centrepiece of Sheherazade, it even occurred to me that the life of a ballet dancer, even though typecast as a eunuch, would be more exciting than that of a medical student. The Company were not encouraging however.

Even today, when I hear the ominous chords of Rimsky-Korsakov that introduce Sheherazade I smell greasepaint (and haemorrhoid ointment), perform a (now arthritic) eunuch waddle, and wonder how life might have been with the Festival Ballet rather than the National Health Service.

# Theodore P Welch

*Theo Welch studied medicine at University College, London and University College Hospital. After training in surgery and obtaining FRCS he worked in Thailand for seven years teaching surgery and then worked as Consultant in the Accident & Emergency Department at Northwick Park Hospital, Harrow. In retirement, he now teaches Clinical Anatomy in Cambridge.*

# Reading Between the Lines

I was born and spent much of my boyhood in China. During the Second World War my family were interned by the Japanese, with about 1,500 others, in a camp in North East China. As the war progressed, food and medicine became in increasingly short supply.

In June 1944, two American men escaped from the camp and linked up with nearby Nationalist (Chiang Kai-shek) Chinese forces. They managed to communicate with one of the internees in the camp using the Chinese 'coolies' who came to empty the camp cesspools. Messages were coded and written on tiny fragments of silk which the coolies carried in their nostrils so they would not be discovered when they were searched. The camp informant told the escapees there were almost no medical supplies left in the camp. The two escapees were able to send a message, sewn into the cloth soles of a messenger's shoes, right across to Congqing in free West China asking for medicines. Four boxes of supplies were parachuted from American planes to local Chinese forces. Getting them into the camp was another matter.

These escapees contacted a friend, Mr Eggar. He worked at the Swiss consulate in Qingdao, a nearby city, and was allowed to visit the camp from time to time. When he saw the boxes, he realised they contained drugs such as the new Sulfas which were not obtainable locally - even the Japanese did not have them. He thought up an ingenious plan and asked his secretary to type up, on embassy notepaper, a list of medicines which were obtainable locally such as aspirin and antiseptics, leaving a four-line space after each item. He then took the list to the head of the Japanese Consular Police for clearance. Although there was some puzzlement at the layout and waste of paper, no objections were raised and the documents were signed and stamped.

Mr Eggar then asked his secretary, using the same typewriter, to insert the names of all the new medicines on the lines between. When Mr Eggar arrived at the camp with the four boxes and the authorisation papers the guards were completely bewildered and were probably mystified as to how approval could have been given for such drugs to be provided for the camp. As everything looked in good order, however, and in order not to lose face, the Camp Commandant stamped the documents and allowed the boxes into the camp. Mr Eggar handed over the life-giving supplies to the grateful doctors and nurses at the hospital.

There is no doubt these much needed supplies saved several lives.

# Sir David Innes Williams

*Sir David Innes Williams was educated at Cambridge and University College Hospital, London. He qualified in 1942 and took resident surgical posts at UCH before joining the Army. In 1944 he served in India as a surgical specialist (Major RAMC). Returning to London he had junior experience at St Peters Hospital and at The Hospital for Sick Children Great Ormond Street before being appointed Urological Surgeon at both these Hospitals. He was effectively the founder of the*  *sub-specialty of paediatric urology and children's work gradually excluded adult practice.*

*He was President of the British Association of Urological Surgeons in 1976 but two years later resigned from his hospitals to become Director of the British Postgraduate Medical Federation and later a Pro-Vice Chancellor in the University of London. He served on the General Medical Council, was Chairman of the Imperial Cancer Research Fund, Vice President of the Royal College of Surgeons, President of the British Medical Association 1988-9 and President of the Royal Society of Medicine 1990-2.*

# A Medico-Legal Experience

Piero was just 11 years old when he was brought to me after a disastrous surgical experience in a small Italian hospital. It seemed that on Christmas Eve he had developed severe abdominal pain, a diagnosis of acute appendicitis was made and he was rushed to hospital. I never found out what preparations were made for operation by either the surgeon or patient, though some fluid restriction might have been useful it turned out!

On opening the abdomen the appendix was found to be only mildly inflamed, but there was a large cystic swelling arising from the pelvis. After enlarging the incision and a meticulous dissection the surgeon removed the 'cyst' complete and unopened but on examining the 'pedicles' was horrified to find the severed ends of the ureters. He had in fact removed a normal full bladder. It was then that the parents lost confidence in local care and brought Piero to London where I embarked on long and not altogether successful reconstructive surgery.

A year later I was asked to go to Italy to give evidence on Piero's behalf and it proved to be a fascinating experience. After being liberally entertained by the Professor from a neighbouring city, who tried unsuccessfully to dictate what I should say, I attended the local Court House to give evidence to an official I judged to be an examining magistrate. Unhappily he did not speak English but he had recruited as an interpreter an endocrinologist whose knowledge of our language was certainly better than his understanding of anatomy. A series of questions was put to me. The first was "When you remove the appendix is it normal to tie off the right ureter?" My succinct reply "NO" did not appear sufficient for the endocrinologist who embarked upon a long speech to the magistrate who then dictated his version to an elderly male, two finger typist, whose first attempts were regularly discarded.

The entire morning was thus taken up by the interrogation and I was glad to escape for lunch with a friend. Expressing the hope that Piero would be handsomely compensated, I received an illuminating but depressing reply. "It will take many many years to decide, the Italian law is as elastic as the scrotal skin."

# Professor H S Wolff

*Heinz Wolff graduated in Physiology and Physics and probably was the first individual to call himself a "Bioengineer". He has worked as the director of Bioengineering Divisions, for the Medical Research Council, at both the National Institute for Medical Research, and the Clinical Research Centre. Whilst serving as the UK delegate on the EC Standing Committee on Biomedical Engineering Research, he coined the phrase "Tools for Living", to describe any technology based device intended to enhance the quality of life of anybody suffering from a disability. In 1983 he founded the self-financing, Institute for Bioengineering at Brunel University, which he directed until 1995. About half of the capacity of the Institute was directed towards the development of Tools for Living, the other half to Space Research.*

*He leads a double life, sharing his professorial duties with those of a scientific entertainer on Radio and TV and as a prolific lecturer. He is now Emeritus Professor of Bioengineering at Brunel University. He is about to start a new career having just been awarded a major grant for a Foresight/LINK project concerned with the use of technology and trained volunteers, to enable old people to stay in their own homes for longer. He intends to go on working until officially declared gaga!*

# The Radio 'Pill'

My introduction to Television about 40 years ago, has a medical origin. At the time I was working at the National Institute for Medical Research, and was presented with the problem of making a radio transmitter small enough to be swallowed and capable of measuring the pressure, wherever it found itself in the gastro-intestinal tract. This "radio pill" was about 8 mm in diameter and 20 mm long, and not particularly difficult to swallow. It would pass out of the stomach within 1 hour and usually pass through the rest of the system within 24-48 hours.

Richard Dimbleby, at that time presenting Panorama, heard about the device, and offered to swallow one, on what was then a live programme. The receiver, which I had provided, tuned not perhaps inappropriately to a frequency close to that used for marine distress messages, translated pressure variations into a varying pitch of an audio note. The pill was duly swallowed, I tuned in to it and to demonstrate that it worked, repeatedly poked Mr Dimbleby in the stomach, producing loud squeals from the receiver. These Teddybear-like squeaks appealed to the nation and ultimately appeared as a track on Richard Dimbleby's commemorative record.

After a few weeks I got my pill back, (it cannot have taken that long) and still treasure it!

# Dr Saleem K. Goolamali

*Saleem Goolamali came to England at the age of 12 and stayed. He was educated in Sussex and received his undergraduate medical training at University College London and University College Hospital Medical School. He is a consultant Dermatologist and works in Harrow, Middlesex. Married with two children, a daughter, a barrister at law and a son who is a doctor.*

# I'm Tired

Yes, I'm tired. For several years I've been blaming it on middle-age, poor blood, lack of vitamins, air pollution, saccharin, obesity, dieting, under arm odour, ear wax build up and another dozen maladies that make you wonder if life is worth living.

But I now find out it isn't that at all.

I'm tired because I'm overworked!

The population of this country is 56 million and 25 million are retired. That leaves 31 million to do all the work. There are 20 million in schools and colleges. That leaves 11 million. Of this total, 2 million are unemployed and 4 million are in the civil service. That leaves 5 million. One million are in the armed services which leaves 4 million to do the work.

Of these, 3 million are employed by County and Borough Councils, leaving 1 million to do the work.

There are 62,000 people in Hospitals and 937,998 people in prison.

That leaves 2 people to do all the work.

You and me.

And you are sitting pretty reading this!

No wonder I'm so tired!